Fürst und Bolf

Aleck and the mutineers of the Bounty

Fürst und Bolf

Aleck and the mutineers of the Bounty

Inktank publishing, 2018

www.inktank-publishing.com

ISBN/EAN: 9783747780930

ALECK,

AND THE

MUTINEERS OF THE BOUNTY;

OR,

THRILLING INCIDENTS

OF

LIFE ON THE OCEAN.

BEING THE

HISTORY OF PITCAIRN'S ISLAND

AND A REMARKABLE ILLUSTRATION OF

THE INFLUENCE OF THE BIBLE.

New Edition, Revised and Enlarged.

BOSTON:
PUBLISHED BY JOHN P. JEWETT & COMPANY.
CLEVELAND, OHIO:
JEWETT, PROCTOR & WORTHINGTON.
1855.

PREFACE.

The following narrative is actual history. The writer supposes every statement he has made, respecting Pitcairn's Island and the colony planted on it, to be in accordance with fact, and is not aware of having added the slightest embellishment to the reality.

The work is designed for the use of the young; but while the author trusts that it will be found highly interesting to them, he hopes that it will be perused with satisfaction by readers of a more advanced age. The child will meet with nothing here so much above comprehension as to be perplexing; and the older person will readily excuse a few passages evidently intended for a younger reader. The book is commended to the candor and kind patronage of all who may wish to promote in the young a love of reading; especially to any who may think it best for youth to seek amusement and instruction, not in the airy regions of fiction, but in the rich field of historic truth. There is reason to fear that the fabulous tales which are often put into the hands of children, have an unhappy tendency, however excellent their morality may be, to create and foster that love for novel-reading which has proved the ruin of multitudes. Many a parent has had occasion to mourn over the melancholy effects produced by the books admitted, without reflection, into the nursery and the sitting-room. The little volume here offered may be considered as an attempt to substitute the narration of facts in the place of fictitious incidents, and to awaken in the mind a desire to know the actual history of real persons and truly existing families and societies, rather than to be simply entertained and perhaps deluded and misguided by contemplating the fancied circumstances of such as the mere offspring of the imagination. The rapid sale of the first edition (consisting of two thousand copies,) of a work adorned with no fascinating attractions of style, and claiming no peculiar merit, other than that of being a true narrative, fully evinces that actual history is eagerly desired by many readers, and perhaps in preference to fiction.

The present edition contains a more full narrative than the first, and continues the history through a longer period, bringing it down, indeed, to the latest accounts received from the island. The contents have been derived from various sources, supposed by the writer to be authentic; among which are, *Barrow's* History of the Mutiny on board the ship Bounty, *Delano's* Voyages, *Shillibeer's* Voyage of the ship Briton, *Beechey's* Narrative of a Voyage to the Pacific and Beering's Strait, the *Naval Biography*, the publications of *Missionary Societies*, and communications of sea captains, and other voyagers, made in a responsible form in newspapers or furnished in manuscript. In drawing from these various sources, the writer has not hesitated to employ freely the language of the different authors without alteration, except for the sake of perspicuity; in some cases the reader is apprized that the language is thus borrowed, in others not, according to convenience in composing the history. The writer feels confident, that whoever may wish for a connected account of the settlement on Pitcairn's Island, will find no where a more complete or faithful one than in this little work.

The principal alterations in this edition relate to the character of Mr. George H. Nobbs, the present acceptable and worthy pastor of the church upon the island.

CONTENTS.

1*

ILLUSTRATIONS.

MUTINEERS OF THE BOUNTY;

OR,

STORY OF ALECK.

CHAPTER I.

INTRODUCTION.

* * * Coral-bottomed isles
That *peaceful* ocean stud, as gems bedeck
A lady's mantle: each the theatre
Of deeds for wonder-waking narrative
And sailor's blithesome tale; but not an isle,
Not e'en the ship-wrecked Crusoe's landing place,
In curious, truthful story well can vie
With ALECK's sunny home. * * *

THE youngest of my readers may not need to be reminded, that in the vast ocean which rolls on the west side of America, and is termed the Pacific, there are numerous islands, some quite large, others very small. But perhaps it will be agreeable to some of them here to take a map of the world, in order to see the ocean and the islands as there marked and named.

One cluster of the islands is called the *Sandwich Isles;* it was here that Captain Cook, who sailed three times round the world, was killed by the savages; but the natives here are not savages now, for pious people in our country some years ago sent to them missionaries, who opened schools for the children, that they might learn to read and write. One of these missionaries published a book containing a very interesting account of the natives of these islands; this book is called Stewart's Journal. The Bible has been translated into their language and printed for their use; meeting-houses have been built, and large numbers of the people have made a public profession of the Christian religion. About the year 1842, they had, under the influence of the Gospel, risen so high in civilization, that they were recognized by the United States, and also by England, as forming an independent state, entitled to hold rank among the nations of the earth. They are now ('54) christianized.

Another cluster of the islands is called the *Society Isles*, and another the *Friendly*. The inhabitants of these were once ignorant and wicked pagans, but are now blessed with schools and Bibles, and ministers who preach the gospel on the Sabbath and other days of the week. Good people of England, about the year 1797, sent to them missionaries, who toiled many years, amid hardships and sufferings, without seeing any fruit of their labors; but at length, in 1815, the most happy results were witnessed. No one can fail to be greatly interested in reading what the missionaries did and suffered, and in learning the story of King Pomare, who became a devoted Christian; some account of these things may be found in Ellis' Polynesian Researches.

In looking upon a map or chart of the Pacific Ocean, the observer will notice, besides groups or clusters of islands, several single ones, as *Christmas Island*, *Sunday Island*, *Pitcairn's Island*. Many of these were not known to the people of England or America before the middle of the last century; some have been discovered more recently. Every year, ships in search of whales sail through the Pacific Ocean far up to the north, even beyond Beering's Straits, between America and Asia; the seamen who have been in these whale ships say, there are *two thousand* more of such islands, which have never been named or put down on any map.

The question has often been asked, both by adults and by children, how there came to be people living on these islands, that stand all alone in the midst of the ocean, hundreds and thousands of miles from the main land. How did they get to the islands?—Where did the people come from? I have been obliged to answer such questions by saying, "I do not know."

Once when this subject was started, I was greatly pleased with the remark of a little girl: "I can tell you, sir," said she. "Can you?" I replied. "Yes, sir, they all came from Adam."

"Pleasant Island, and many others in the Pacific, are infested by Europeans who are either runaway convicts, expirees, or deserters from whalers, and are for the most part men of the very worst description, who, it appears, prefer living a precarious life of indolence and ease with the unenlightened savage, rather than submit to the restraint of the salutary laws of civilized society; they live in a manner easily to be imagined from men of this class, without either law, religion, or education, to control them, with an unlimited quantity of ardent spirits, which they obtain from distilling a liquor that exudes from the cocoanut tree. This spirit is not very palatable, but it serves, to use their own expression, to tickle the brain; when under the influence of intoxication the most atrocious crimes are committed by these miscreants, who must, both by their pernicious example and advice, do much injury to this naturally mild and well disposed race of men, and will retard considerably the great work of civilization and Christianity, whenever those blessings are offered them by the servants of God. These fiends frequently urge the different tribes to war and deeds of blood, in order to participate in the spoils of the vanquished.

The island to which I refer, is called *Pitcairn's*. This island was discovered in 1767, by the navigator Carteret. He first saw it on Thursday, the 2d of July. Upon his approaching it the next day, it appeared like a rock rising out of the sea, and seemed to be uninhabited. It was covered with trees, and a small stream of fresh water was running down one side of it. He desired to land upon it, but the surf of the ocean broke with such violence upon the shore that he could not do it. A great number of sea-birds were hovering about it, and there seemed to be fish playing in the waters around it. The island rose so high above the surface of the ocean, that it was seen at a distance of more than forty miles. The person who first perceived it, was a young man by the name of Pitcairn, and therefore it was called Pitcairn's island. It is about six miles long and three wide. Captain Carteret described it as being in latitude 25° south, and longitude 133° west from Greenwich. More correct observations have shown it to be in latitude 25° 4′ south, and longitude 130° 25′ west. A view of its appearance as drawn by an actual observer, (Lieutenant Shillibeer,) is given on page 11.

I believe that the people in Europe and America never heard anything more about this island for above forty years, and then an American ship accidentally visited the place. It was the ship Topaz, commanded by Captain Folger, who, some time afterwards, ceased going to sea, and about the year 1828 was residing, as I have heard, in the State of Ohio. He was on a voyage to procure seal skins to carry to China, and in the month of February, 1808, approached Pitcairn's island, supposing it to be without inhabitants. As he was going to the shore in his boat, he was met by three young men in a canoe, and was filled with surprise, when they addressed him in the English language, and asked who he was. He told them he was from America: this they did not fully understand, and with great earnestness said, "You come from America? Where is America? Is it in Ireland?"

Captain Folger then asked them, "Who are you?" "We are Englishmen." "Where were you born?" "On that island, which you see." "How then are you Englishmen, if you were born on that island, which the English never possessed?" "Because our father was an Englishman." "Who is your father?" With great simplicity they answered—"Aleck." "Who is Aleck?" said Captain Folger. They only replied, "Don't you know Aleck?"

This conversation awakened the captain's curiosity, so that he was very desirous to learn the history of these islanders, and he requested the young men to go and tell Aleck, that the master of the ship wished to see him, and would give him anything he might want, if he would come on board. But Aleck was unwilling to do

Pitcairn's Island.

it, probably being afraid that the ship was from England, and that the design was to take and carry him to that country; and in the end we shall learn what reason he had to fear this. The captain therefore went on shore, spent several hours in conversation with Aleck, and ascertained that he was indeed an Englishman, properly named Alexander Smith, from the city of London, and that he had been upon the island about eighteen years. He learned also that there were, besides the young men, between thirty and forty women and children under the direction and government of Aleck or Smith; although the island had no inhabitant on Smith's arrival, and no ship or canoe had afterwards visited it, before Captain Folger. Another remarkable thing was, that these persons all spoke two different languages, the English and the Otaheitan or Tahitian.

The reader will, no doubt, be as desirous to know the history of this little nation as Captain Folger was; and I shall endeavor to gratify the desire, although I must relate some things that were very wicked.

CHAPTER II.

THE BREAD-TREE.

* * * "They told of climes
Where unsown fields a plenteous harvest yield,
Where bread itself by nature's generous hand
Is kneaded, and on trees in golden loaves
Hangs thick. * * * *
* * * * *
'T was food for freemen only meant; since when
Fell avarice would the precious tree transplant
To lands with slavery's galling yoke oppressed,
That wish, by Providence, was strangely foiled
Through human crime, or through the fatal blight
By Heaven's curse upon the tyrant's soil."

In order to give the full history, it will be necessary first to mention a very singular kind of fruit tree, that grows wild upon the islands in the Pacific Ocean, and flourishes especially on the Sandwich Isles and the Society Isles. It is the *bread-tree*. It is, when full grown, as large as the walnut tree in America, and stands upright, being sometimes sixty feet high, with a trunk between two and three feet in diameter. Its wood is soft, and of a yellowish color; if wounded, it pours out a milky, glutinous liquor. Its leaves are oval in shape, bright green, and sometimes eighteen inches long, and eleven or twelve wide. It bears a large circular fruit, about six inches in thickness; or, as another describes it, "of the size and shape of a child's head." It grows at the end of the branches, to which it is attached by a short thick stalk. A view of a small branch with the fruit is seen on page 15, as given by Mr. Ellis. The fruit is covered with a thin skin, of pale green, marked with regular lines forming small six-sided figures; when it is fully ripe, the color is a rich yellow. It has a "core as big as the handle of a knife." The part between the skin and the core is a substance, white, pure, sweet, juicy, and about as soft as new bread; this part is good to eat, and is used instead of bread, and therefore the tree is called *bread-tree.* To procure this food it is only necessary to climb the tree and pluck the fruit, throw it upon hot coals and roast it, then take off the skin, and there is a "beautiful, light colored, smoking loaf." It tastes a little like wheat bread, but more like the hard boiled yolk of an egg. *Three* trees will bear fruit enough to supply one man with food.

As long ago as the year 1688, the navigator Dampier described it as follows: "The bread-fruit, as we call it, grows on a large tree, as big and high as our largest apple-trees; it hath a spreading head, full of branches and dark leaves. The fruit grows on the boughs like apples; it is as big as a penny loaf, when wheat is at five shillings a bushel; it is of a round shape and hath a thick tough rind; when the fruit is ripe it is yellow and soft, and the taste is sweet and pleasant. The natives of Guam use it for bread. They gather it when full grown, while it is green and hard; then they bake it in an oven, which scorcheth the rind and makes it black, but they scrape off the outside black crust and there remains a thin tender crust, and the inside is soft,

2

tender and white, like the crumb of a penny loaf." Captain Cook corroborated this account, in substance, and it is not surprising, therefore, that the English merchants and planters, and others who had possessions in the West Indies, were desirous to introduce into these islands this remarkable tree,—

"The bread-tree, which, without the plough-share, yields
The unreaped harvest of unfurrowed fields,
And bakes its unadulterated loaves
Without a furnace in unpurchased groves,
And flings off famine from its fertile breast,
A priceless market for the gathering guest."

In consequence of the representations of these merchants, planters and others interested, King George the Third gave authority, in the year 1787, for an expedition for procuring plants to be carried to the islands in the West Indies, that the bread-fruit might there furnish a cheap and wholesome food for the black slave population. To accomplish this object, the government fitted out, under the careful superintendence of Sir Joseph Banks, a vessel, called the Bounty, having on board forty-four officers and sailors, and two gardeners who were to take care of the plants. The Bounty, commanded by Lieutenant Bligh, sailed from England the 23d of December, 1787, and on the 26th of October, 1788, arrived at Otaheite, or Tahiti, the largest of the Society Isles, and came to anchor in Matavai Bay; having run over, according to the log, after leaving England, a distance of twenty-seven thousand and eighty-six miles. Lieutenant Bligh staid there twenty-three weeks, being very kindly treated by the natives, and procured more than a thousand bread-fruit plants, which were carefully nourished in a garden of pots on board the vessel. The natives visited the ship as soon as she was anchored, and many inquiries were made after Captain Cook, Sir Joseph Banks, and others who had previously been at the island. The people were at that time in a state of great ignorance, the missionaries, that I have before mentioned, not having been sent thither until some years afterwards. Lieutenant Bligh allowed his men to form improper intimacies with them; by

Branch of the Bread Tree.

which the virtue of many simple-hearted youth was most grossly and wickedly corrupted; a base return for the hospitality and kindness of the islanders. The longer the foreigners remained, the more they had occasion to be grateful, it is said. In every house they wished to enter they always experienced a kind reception. The Otaheitans, we are told, have the most perfect easiness of manner, equally free from forwardness and formality; and that "there is a candor and sincerity about them that is quite delightful. When they offer refreshments, for instance, if they are not accepted they do not think of offering them a second time; for they have not the least idea of that ceremonious kind of refusal which expects a second invitation." "Having one day," says Bligh, "exposed myself too much to the sun, I was taken ill, on which all the powerful people, both men and women, collected around me, offering their assistance. For this short illness I was made ample amends by the pleasure I received from the attention and appearance of affection in these kind people."

On one occasion the Bounty had nearly gone ashore in a tremendous gale of wind, and on another did actually get aground; on both which accidents these kind-hearted people came in crowds to congratulate the captain on her escape; and many of them are stated to have been affected in the most lively manner, shedding tears, while the danger in which the ship was placed continued.

On the 9th December, the surgeon of the Bounty died, from the effects of intemperance and indolence. This unfortunate man is represented to have been in a constant state of intoxication, and was so averse from any kind of exercise that he never could be prevailed on to take half a dozen hours upon deck at a time in the whole course of the voyage. Lieutenant Bligh had obtained permission to bury him on shore; and on going with the chief, Tinah, to the spot intended for his burial-place, "I found," says he, "the natives had already begun to dig his grave." Tinah asked if they were doing it right. "There," says he, "the sun rises, and there it sets." Whether the idea of making the grave east and west is their own, or whether they learned it from the Spaniards who buried the captain of their ship on the island in 1774, there were no means of ascertaining; but it was certain they had no intimation of that kind from anybody belonging to the Bounty. When the funeral took place, the chiefs and many of the natives attended the ceremony, and showed great attention during the service. Many of the principal natives attended divine service on Sundays, and behaved with great decency. Some of the women at one time betrayed an inclination to laugh at the general responses; but the captain says, on looking at them they appeared much ashamed.

By the 31st of March, 1789, all the plants were on board, being in seven hundred and seventy-four pots, thirty-nine tubs, and twenty-four boxes. The number of bread-fruit plants were one thousand and fifteen; besides which there were collected a number of other plants: the *avee*, which is one of the finest flavored fruits in the world; the *ayyah*, which is a fruit not so rich, but of a fine flavor, and very refreshing; the *rattah*, not much unlike a chestnut, which grows on a large tree in great quantities; they are singly, in large pods, from one to two inches broad, and may be eaten raw, or boiled in the same manner as Windsor beans, and so dressed are equally good; the *orai-ab*, which is a very superior kind of plantain. "All these," says Bligh, "I was particularly recommended to collect by my worthy friend Sir Joseph Banks."

The Bounty sailed from Tahiti on the 4th of April, 1789, to carry the plants to the West Indies, but never reached those islands; the object of introducing there the bread-tree was therefore not accomplished by this expedition. The vessel continued on her voyage prosperously for several days, passing by a number of different islands in the Pacific Ocean. On the morning of the 28th of April, when she was sailing near the island Tofoa, one of the Friendly Isles, some of the men suddenly rose against the commander in a mutiny, which is described as one of the most atrocious ever committed. They entered his cabin before sunrise, while he was yet asleep, drew him out of the bed, tied his hands behind his back, and threatened him with instant death if he should speak, or make the least noise. He made several efforts to bring them to a sense of their duty, but it only called forth curses and threats from the guard, that stood around him armed with loaded guns and bayonets.

Lieutenant Bligh and all the men, whom the mutineers wished to get rid of, were then forced into the boat belonging to the vessel, and cast adrift in the open ocean. The boat was only twenty-three feet long, not quite seven feet wide, and not quite three feet deep, yet into this little space were crowded nineteen persons. They received for provisions only twenty-eight gallons of water, a small quantity of rum and wine, one hundred and fifty pounds of bread, and a few pieces of pork. Thus situated, they passed forty-seven days of extreme danger and suffering. At length, on the 14th of June, they reached, in their boat, a settlement of the Dutch at Coupang, on the island Timor, in the East Indian sea, between Borneo and New Holland.

On their arrival they appeared like ghastly spectres. Their bodies were reduced to skin and bone, their limbs were full of sores, and they were clothed in rags. In this condition, while tears of joy and gratitude were flowing down their cheeks, the people of Timor beheld them with a mixture of horror, surprise, and pity. Twelve of them lived through their hardships, and receiving every necessary aid from the Dutch governor, at last reached their native country.

Lieutenant Bligh arrived in England in March, 1790. The next year he went out again after the bread-fruit, and succeeded in carrying many plants to the West Indies, where the tree now grows in considerable abundance, although it has not met the expectation of those who introduced it as a means of supplying food. He was afterwards promoted to a higher command, and became an admiral in the English navy.

The reader may wish to know more of the details of the mutiny, and the wonderful voyage in the open boat. I will, therefore, in the next chapters, give some particulars from Lieutenant Bligh's journal and other sources.

CHAPTER III.

THE MUTINY.

"'T is pride begets in man the hell he feels
Within him; hence proceeds rash violence,
The pirate's mutiny, the rebel's war
Against just rule of man; and hence the strife
In sinful hearts that hate the law of love,
Their Maker's will defying." * * *
* * Of worse deeds worse sufferings must ensue."

"Just before sunrising on Tuesday the 28th, while I was yet asleep," says Lieutenant Bligh in his journal, "Mr. Christian, officer of the watch, Charles Churchill, ship's corporal, John Mills, gunner's mate, and Thomas Burkitt, seaman, came into my cabin, and seizing me, tied my hands with a cord behind my back, threatening me with instant death if I spoke or made the least noise. I called, however, as loud as I could, in hopes of assistance; but they had already secured the officers who were not of their party, by placing sentinels at their doors. There were three men at my cabin-door, besides the four within; Christian had only a cutlass in his hand, the others had muskets and bayonets. I was hauled out of bed, and forced on deck in my shirt, suffering great pain from the tightness with which they had tied my hands behind my back, held by Fletcher Christian, and Charles Churchill, with a bayonet at my breast, and two men, Alexander Smith and Thomas Burkitt, behind me, with loaded muskets cocked and bayonets fixed. [This scene is represented in the cut on page 21.] I demanded the reason of such violence, but received no other answer than abuse for not holding my tongue. The master, the gunner, Mr. Elphinstone the master's mate, and Nelson, were kept confined below; and the fore-hatchway was guarded by sentinels. The boatswain and carpenter, and also Mr. Samuel the clerk, were allowed to come upon deck, where they saw me standing abaft the mizzenmast, with my hands tied behind my back, under a guard, with Christian at their head.

"The boatswain was ordered to hoist the launch out, with a threat, that if he did not do it instantly, to take care of himself. When the boat was out, Mr. Hayward and Mr. Hallet, two of the midshipmen, and Mr. Samuel, were ordered into it. I demanded what their intention was in giving this order, and endeavored to persuade the people near me not to persist in such acts of violence; but it was to no effect—'Hold your tongue, sir, or you are dead this instant,' was constantly repeated to me. The master by this time had sent to request that he might come on deck, which was permitted; but he was soon ordered back again to his cabin.

"I continued my endeavors to turn the tide of affairs, when Christian changed the cutlass which he had in his hand for a bayonet that was brought to him, and holding me with a strong gripe by the cord that tied my hands, he threatened, with many oaths, to kill me immediately, if I would not be quiet; the villains round me had their pieces cocked and bayonets fixed. Particular persons were called on to go into the boat, and were hurried over the side; whence I concluded that with these people I was to be set adrift. I therefore made another effort to bring about a change, but with no other effect than to be threatened with having my brains blown out.

"The boatswain and seamen who were to go in the boat were allowed to collect twine, canvass, lines, sails, cordage, an eight-and-twenty gallon cask of water; and Mr. Samuel got one hundred and fifty pounds of bread, with a small quantity of rum and wine, also a quadrant and compass; but he was forbidden, on pain of death, to touch either map, ephemeris, book of astronomical observations, sextant, timekeeper, or any of my surveys or drawings.

"The mutineers having forced those of the seamen whom they meant to get rid of into the boat, Christian directed a dram to be served to each of his own crew. I then unhappily saw that nothing could be done to effect the recovery of the ship: there was no one to

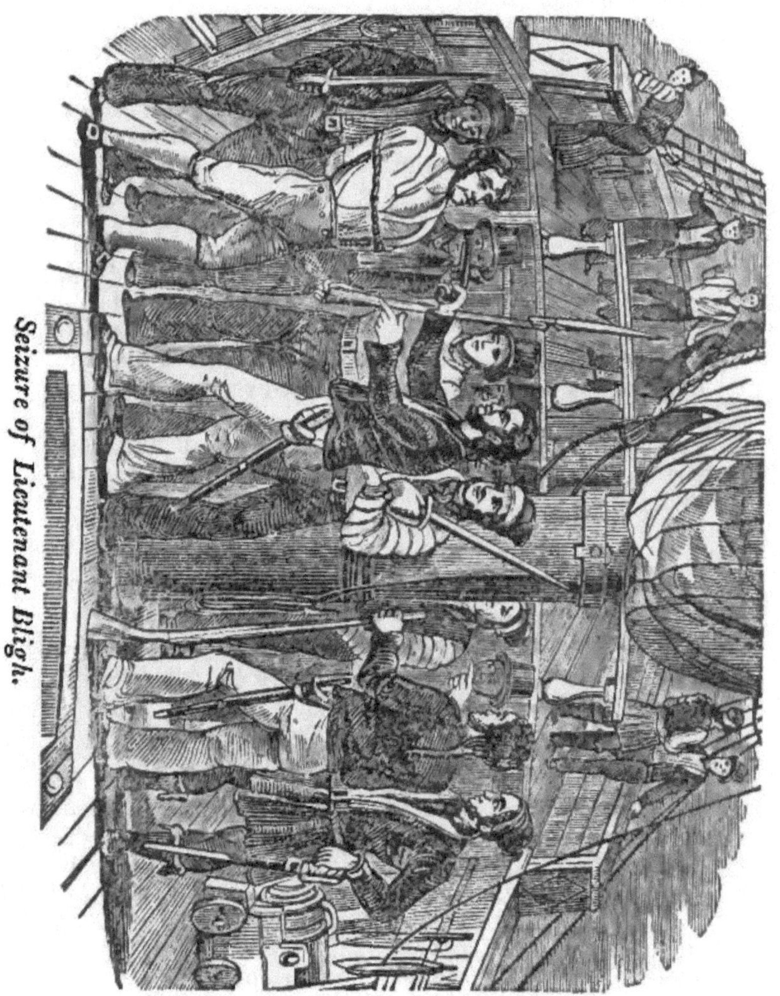

Seizure of Lieutenant Bligh.

assist me, and every endeavor on my part was answered with threats of death.

"The officers were next called upon deck, and forced over the side into the boat, while I was kept apart from every one, abaft the mizzenmast; Christian, armed with a bayonét, holding me by the bandage that secured my hands. The guard round me had their pieces cocked, but on my daring the ungrateful wretches to fire, they uncocked them.

"Isaac Martin, one of the guard over me, I saw had an inclination to assist me, and as he fed me with shaddock (my lips being quite parched) we explained our wishes to each other by our looks; but this being observed, Martin was removed from me. He then attempted to leave the ship, for which purpose he got into the boat; but with many threats they obliged him to return. The armorer, Joseph Coleman, and two of the carpenters, M'Intosh and Norman, were also kept contrary to their inclination; and they begged of me, after I was astern in the boat, to remember that they declared they had no hand in the transaction. Michael Byrne, I am told, likewise wanted to leave the ship.

"It is of no moment for me to recount my endeavors to bring back the offenders to a sense of their duty; all I could do was by speaking to them in general; but it was to no purpose, for I was kept securely bound, and no one except the guard suffered to come near me. To Mr. Samuel (clerk) I am indebted for securing my journals and commission, with some material ship papers. Without these I had nothing to certify what I had done, and my honor and character might have been suspected, without my possessing a proper document to have defended them. All this he did with great resolution, though guarded and strictly watched.

"It appeared to me that Christian was some time in doubt whether he should keep the carpenter or his mates; at length he determined on the latter, and the carpenter was ordered into the boat. He was permitted, but not without some opposition, to take his tool-chest. Much altercation took place among the mutinous crew during the whole business. As for Christian, he seemed as if meditating destruction on himself and every one else. I asked for arms, but they laughed at me, and said I was well acquainted with the people among whom I was going, and therefore did not want them; four cutlasses, however, were thrown into the boat after we were veered astern.

"The officers and men being in the boat, they only waited for me, of which the master-at-arms informed Christian; who then said, 'Come, Captain Bligh, your officers and men are now in the boat, and you must go with them; if you attempt to make the least resistance you will instantly be put to death;' and without further ceremony, with a tribe of armed ruffians about me, I was forced over the side, when they untied my hands. Being in the boat, we were veered astern by a rope. A few pieces of pork were thrown to us, and some clothes, also the cutlasses I have already mentioned; and it was then that the armorer and carpenters called out to me to remember that they had no hand in the transaction. After having undergone a great deal of ridicule, and been kept for some time to make sport for these unfeeling wretches, we were at length cast adrift in the open ocean.

"I had with me in the boat the following persons:—

John Fryer, *Master;* Thomas Ledward, *Acting Surgeon;* David Nelson, *Botanist;* William Peckover, *Gunner;* William Cole, *Boatswain;* William Purcell, *Carpenter;* William Elphinstone, *Master's Mate;* Thomas Hayward and John Hallet, *Midshipmen;* John Norton and Peter Lenkletter, *Quarter-masters;* Lawrence Lebogue, *Sailmaker;* John Smith and Thomas Hall, *Cooks;* George Simpson, *Quarter-master's Mate;* Robert Tinkler, *a Boy;* Robert Lamb, *Butcher;* Mr. Samuel, *Clerk.* In all eighteen.

"There remained in the Bounty:

Fletcher Christian, *Master's Mate;* Peter Heywood, Edward Young, and George Stewart, *Midshipmen;* Charles Churchill, *Master-at-arms;* John Mills, *Gunner's Mate;* James Morrison, *Boatswain's Mate;* Thomas Burkitt, Matthew Quintal, John Sumner, John Millward, William M'Koy, Henry Hillbrant, Michael Byrne, William Musprat, Alexander Smith, John Williams, Thomas Ellison, Isaac Martin, Richard Skinner, and Matthew Thompson, *Able Seamen;* William Brown, *Gardener;* Joseph Coleman, *Armorer;* Charles Norman, *Carpenter's Mate;* Thomas M'Intosh, *Carpenter's Crew.* In all twenty-five—and the most able of the ship's company.

"Notwithstanding the roughness with which I was treated, the remembrance of past kindnesses produced some signs of remorse in Christian. When they were forcing me out of the ship, I asked him if this treatment was a proper return for the many instances he had received of my friendship. He appeared disturbed at my question, and answered, with much emotion, 'That, Captain Bligh, that is the thing;—I am in hell!—I am in hell!'

"As soon as I had time to reflect, I felt an inward satisfaction, which prevented any depression of my spirits: conscious of my integrity and anxious solicitude for the good of the service in which I had been engaged, I found my mind wonderfully supported, and I began to conceive hopes, notwithstanding so heavy a calamity, that I should one day be able to account to my king and country for the misfortune. A few hours before my situation had been peculiarly flattering. I had a ship in the most perfect order, and well stored with every necessary both for service and health; by early attention to those particulars, I had, as much as lay in my power, provided against any accident in case I could not get through Endeavor Straits, as well as against what might befall me in them; add to this, the plants had been successfully preserved in the most flourishing state: so that, upon the whole, the voyage was two thirds completed, and the remaining part, to all appearance, in a very promising way; every person on board being in perfect health, to establish which was ever among the principal objects of my attention.

"It will very naturally be asked, What could be the reason for such a revolt? In answer to which I can only conjecture, that the mutineers had flattered themselves with the hopes of a more happy life among the Otaheitans than they could possibly enjoy in England; and this, joined to some female connexions, most probably occasioned the whole transaction. The ship, indeed, while within our sight, steered to the W. N. W.; but I considered this only as a feint, for when we were sent away, 'Huzza for Otaheite!' was frequently heard among the mutineers.

"The women of Otaheite are handsome, mild and cheerful in their manners and conversation, possessed of great sensibility, and have sufficient delicacy to make them admired and beloved. The chiefs were so much attached to our people, that they rather encouraged their stay among them than otherwise, and even made them promises of large possessions. Under these and many other attendant circumstances, equally desirable, it is now perhaps not so much to be wondered at, though scarcely possible to have been foreseen, that a set of sailors, most of them void of connexions, should be led away; especially when, in addition to such powerful inducements, they imagined it in their power to fix themselves in the midst of plenty, on one of the finest islands in the world, where they need not labor, and where the allurements of dissipation are beyond anything that can be conceived. The utmost, however, that any commander could have supposed to have happened is, that some of the people would have been tempted to desert.

"Desertions have happened, more or less, from most of the ships that have been at the Society Islands; but it has always been in the commanders' power to make the chiefs return their people; the knowledge, therefore, that it was unsafe to desert, perhaps first led mine to consider with what ease so small a ship might be surprised, and that so favorable an opportunity would never offer to them again.

"The secrecy of this mutiny is beyond all conception. Thirteen of the party, who were with me, had always lived forward among the seamen; yet neither they, nor the messmates of Christian, Stewart, Heywood, and Young, had ever observed any circumstance that made them in the least suspect what was going on. To such a close-planned act of villany, my mind being entirely free from any suspicion, it is not wonderful that I fell a sacrifice. Perhaps, if there had been marines on board, a sentinel at my cabin-door might have prevented it; for I slept with the door always open, that the officer of the watch might have access to me on all occasions, the possibility of such a conspiracy being ever the furthest from

3

my thoughts. Had their mutiny been occasioned by any grievances, either real or imaginary, I must have discovered symptoms of their discontent, which would have put me on my guard: but the case was far otherwise. Christian, in particular, I was on the most friendly terms with: that very day he was engaged to have dined with me; and the preceding night he excused himself from supping with me, on pretence of being unwell; for which I felt concerned, having no suspicions of his integrity and honor."

Such is the account of the mutiny published by Lieutenant Bligh immediately on his return to England, and his story obtained implicit credit. But it has been since proved that in some particulars he was mistaken, and especially that his conjecture as to the reason for the mutiny was erroneous. He was a man, it is said, of very irritable temper; during the voyage there had been repeated misunderstandings between him and his officers; on several occasions he had given them and the seamen just reasons for complaint. The master, Mr. Fryer, and the master's mate, Fletcher Christian, are said to have had much cause for dissatisfaction; but there was no general discontent among the crew, and the mutiny was not the result of a preconcerted conspiracy, but the effect of a sudden phrensy of passion in Christian. He was unfortunately under some obligations to Lieutenant Bligh of a pecuniary nature, of which Bligh frequently reminded him when a difference arose; this taunt was, of course, exceedingly irritating to a young man of haughty feelings. But whatever may have been the mistakes or the severity of the commander, no excuse can be found to exculpate the guilty mutineers. According to a journal which was kept by James Morrison, who was boatswain's mate, Christian was greatly provoked by what occurred in the afternoon of the day before the mutiny. In the afternoon of the 27th, Lieutenant Bligh came upon deck, and missing some of the cocoanuts which had been piled up between the guns, said they had been stolen, and could not have been taken away without the knowledge of the officers, all of whom were sent for and questioned on the subject.

On their declaring that they had not seen any of the people touch them, he exclaimed, "Then you must have taken them yourselves;" and proceeded to inquire of them separately how many they had purchased. On coming to Mr. Christian, that gentleman answered, "I do not know, sir; but I hope you do not think me so mean as to be guilty of stealing yours." Mr. Bligh replied, with an oath, "Yes, I do—you must have stolen them from me, or you would be able to give a better account of them;" then turning to the other officers, he said, with another oath, "You scoundrels, you are all thieves alike, and combine with the men to rob me. I suppose you will steal my yams next; but I 'll sweat you for it, you rascals—I 'll make half of you jump overboard before you get through Endeavor Straits." This threat was followed by an order to the clerk "to stop the villains' grog, and give them but half a pound of yams to-morrow; if they steal them, I 'll reduce them to a quarter."

This was more than Christian could bear; but Lieutenant Bligh, having vented his rage in this manner about the cocoanuts, seems, as often happens with men whose temper gets the better of their reason, to have become calm immediately afterwards; he invited Christian to sup with him in the cabin the same evening, evidently wishing to renew a friendly intercourse; happy for all parties it might have been, if the invitation had been accepted. Christian, however, declined, on the plea of being unwell; the commander, probably sorry for his ebullition of anger, and intent on soothing the feelings he had wounded, invited Christian to dine with him the next day, and in his own journal, (without noticing the quarrel about the cocoanuts,) he writes as if Christian had signified his acceptance of the latter invitation. But the exasperated mate was meditating other things. The 27th of April closed with one of those beautiful nights which characterize the tropical regions, when, after a scorching day, the air breathes a most refreshing coolness, and the stillness of nature disposes the mind to reflection; the moon, then in the first quarter, was shedding her soft light along the surface of the sea, and a gentle breeze scarcely rippled the water. Toward ten o'clock, Bligh came on deck, as was his custom, before retiring to sleep; Fryer, the master, had the watch; in a short and quiet conversation, they congratulated themselves on the pleasing prospect of fine weather and a full moon to light them through the dangers of Endeavor Straits, and a happy termination of their voyage. On that same lovely night, Christian, pondering over his grievances, stung with the recent insult, contemplating the quiet water, and looking to the island Tofoa then in sight, resolved to escape from a condition which now seemed to him intolerable, and suddenly formed the singular project of escaping to that island upon a raft. The raft was immediately constructed by fastening some staves to a stout plank, and various articles of trade, such as nails and beads, and some food, were put into a bag to take with him. Finding that he could not effect his object during the first and middle watches, as he himself afterwards related, he laid down to rest about half past three in the morning. Scarcely had he fallen asleep when, at four o'clock, he was called by midshipman Stewart to relieve the deck and take the third or morning watch; Stewart had been informed by Christian of his intention, and now urged him to abandon it. Christian then took charge of the deck, and seeing midshipman Hayward, the mate of his watch, lie down to sleep, and finding that midshipman Hallet, the other mate of his watch, did not appear, the thought of seizing the ship came into his mind; he instantly resolved to do it, and at once disclosed his scheme to several of the seamen who had been flogged with the cat, who readily joined him. The keys of the arm-chest were obtained from Coleman the armorer under pretence of wanting a musket to fire at a shark then alongside. Thus it appears that no conspiracy existed, but the mutiny was suddenly conceived by the hot-headed Fletcher Christian, smarting under the wounds his pride had received, and bent upon escaping from a condition that seemed to him no longer tolerable. It is astonishing that he should have succeeded in exciting, thus, in an hour, a mutiny so fatally successful.

The only officer that tried to bring the mutineers to a sense of their duty was Mr. Fryer, the master, who deserves the more credit for his conduct, as Lieutenant Bligh had given him, it is said, the greatest cause for discontent, having been more severe to him than to any other officer. Mr. Fryer, who was forced into the boat with the commander, and lived to reach England, gave in court the following account, in substance: that he was relieved from his watch at twelve o'clock, and retired, leaving all quiet; that at dawn of day he was greatly alarmed by an unusual noise; and that, on attempting to jump up, John Sumner and Matthew Quintal laid their hands upon his breast and desired him to lie still, saying he was their prisoner; that on expostulating with them, he was told, " Hold your tongue, or you are a dead man; but if you remain quiet, there is none on board will hurt a hair of your head." He farther deposes, that on raising himself on the locker, he saw on the ladder, going upon deck, Mr. Bligh in his shirt, with his hands tied behind him, and Christian holding him by the cord; that the master-at-arms, Churchill, then came to his cabin and took a brace of pistols and a hanger, saying, " I will take care of these, Mr. Fryer;" that he asked, on seeing Mr. Bligh bound, what they were going to do with the captain; that Sumner replied, with an oath, " Put him into the boat, and let the —— see if he can live upon three fourths of a pound of yams a day;" that he remonstrated with such conduct, but in vain; they said he must go in the small cutter; " The small cutter!" Mr. Fryer exclaimed; " why her bottom is almost out, and very much eaten by the worms!" to which Sumner and Quintal both said, with a profane oath, " the boat is too good for him;" that after much entreaty he prevailed on them to ask Christian if he might be allowed to go on deck, which after some hesitation was granted. "When I came on deck," says Mr. Fryer, "Mr. Bligh was standing by the mizzenmast with his hands tied behind him, and Christian holding the cord with one hand and a bayonet in the other. I said, " Christian, consider what you are about." "Hold your tongue, sir," he

3*

said; "I have been in hell for two weeks past; Captain Bligh has brought all this on himself." I told him that Mr. Bligh and he not agreeing was no reason for taking the ship. "Hold your tongue, sir," he said. I said, "Mr. Christian, you and I have been on friendly terms during the voyage, therefore give me leave to speak,—let Mr. Bligh go down to his cabin, and I make no doubt we shall all be friends again:" he then repeated, "Hold your tongue, sir; it is too late;" and threatening me if I said anything more. Mr. Fryer then asked him to give a better boat than the cutter; he said, "No, that boat is good enough." Bligh now said to the master, that the man behind the hencoops (Isaac Martin) was his friend, and desired him (the master) to knock Christian down, which Christian must have heard, but took no notice; Mr. Fryer then attempted to get past Christian to speak to Martin, but he put his bayonet to his breast, saying, "Sir, if you advance an inch farther I will run you through;" and ordered two armed men to take him down to his cabin. Shortly afterward he was desired to go on deck, when Christian ordered him into the boat: he said, "I will stay with you, if you will give me leave." "No, sir," he replied, "go directly into the boat." Bligh, then on the gangway, said, "Mr. Fryer, stay in the ship." "No, sir," Christian said, using the name of God profanely, "go into the boat or I will run you through." Mr. Fryer states, that during this time very bad language was used by the people towards Mr. Bligh; that with great difficulty they prevailed on Christian to suffer a few articles to be put into the boat. On being asked what he supposed Christian meant when he said he had been in hell for a fortnight, Fryer said he supposed him to refer to the abuse he had received from Mr. Bligh, and the frequent quarrels they had; and mentioned, that the day before the mutiny, Mr. Bligh had challenged all the young gentlemen and the people with stealing his cocoanuts.

But here we will drop the subject of the mutiny, and, in the next chapter, follow the boat in its perilous voyage.

CHAPTER IV.

THE VOYAGE IN THE BOAT.

"The launch is crowded with the faithful few
That wait their chief—a melancholy crew:
But some remain'd reluctant on the deck
Of that proud vessel, now a moral wreck—
And view'd their captain's fate with piteous eyes;
While others scoff'd his augur'd miseries,
Sneer'd at the prospect of the pigmy sail,
And the slight bark, so laden and so frail."

THE first consideration of Lieutenant Bligh and his eighteen unfortunate companions, on being cast adrift in their open boat, was to examine the state of their resources. The quantity of provisions which they found to have been thrown into the boat by some few kind-hearted messmates, amounted to one hundred and fifty pounds of bread, sixteen pieces of pork, each weighing two pounds, six quarts of rum, six bottles of wine, with twenty-eight gallons of water, and four empty barricoes. Being so near to the island of Tofoa, it was resolved to seek there a supply of bread-fruit and water, to preserve, if possible, the above-mentioned stock entire; but after rowing along the coast, they discovered only some cocoanut-trees on the top of high precipices, from which, with much danger, owing to the surf, and great difficulty in climbing the cliffs, they succeeded in obtaining about twenty nuts. The second day they made excursions into the island, but without success. They met, however, with a few natives, who came down with them to the cove where the boat was lying; and others presently followed. They made inquiries after the ship, and Bligh unfortunately advised they should say that the ship had overset and sunk, and that they only were saved. The story might be innocent, but it was certainly indiscreet to put the people in possession of their defenceless situation; however, they brought in small quantities of bread-fruit, plantains, and cocoanuts, but little or no water could be procured. These supplies, scanty as they were, served to keep up the spirits of the men: "They no longer," says Bligh, "regarded me with those anxious looks which had constantly been directed towards me since we lost sight of the ship: every countenance appeared to have a degree of cheerfulness, and they all seemed determined to do their best."

The numbers of the natives having so much increased as to line the whole beach, they began knocking stones together, which was known to be the preparatory signal for an attack. With some difficulty, on account of the surf, our seamen succeeded in getting the things that were on shore into the boat, together with all the men, except John Norton, quarter-master, who was casting off the stern-fast. The natives immediately rushed upon this poor man, and actually stoned him to death. A volley of stones was also discharged at the boat, and every one in it was more or less hurt. This induced the people to push out to sea with all the speed they were able to give to the launch, but to their surprise and alarm, several canoes filled with stones followed close after them and renewed the attack; against which, the only return the unfortunate men in the boat could make, was with the stones of the assailants that lodged in her, a species of warfare in which they were very inferior to the Indians. The only expedient left was to tempt the enemy to desist from the pursuit, by throwing overboard some clothes, which fortunately induced the canoes to stop and pick them up; and night coming on they returned to the shore, leaving the party in the boat to reflect on their unhappy situation.

The men now entreated their commander to take them towards home; and on being told that no hope of relief could be entertained till they reached Timor, a distance of full twelve hundred leagues, they all readily agreed to be content with an allowance, which, on calculation of their resources, the commander informed them would not exceed one ounce of bread and a quarter of a pint of water per day. Recommending them, therefore, in the most solemn manner, not to depart from their promise in this respect, "we bore away," says Bligh, "across a sea where the navigation is but little known, in a small boat, twenty-three feet long from stem to stern, deeply laden with eighteen men. I was happy, however, to see that every one seemed better satisfied with our situation than myself. It was about eight o'clock at night on the 2d May when we bore away under a reefed lug-foresail; and having divided the people into watches, and got the boat into a little order, we returned thanks to God for our miraculous preservation, and in full confidence of his gracious support, I found my mind more at ease than it had been for some time past."

At daybreak on the 3d, the forlorn and almost hopeless navigators saw with alarm the sun to rise fiery and red,—a sure indication of a severe gale of wind; and, accordingly, at eight o'clock it blew a violent storm, and the sea ran so very high, that the sail was becalmed when between the seas, and too much to have set when on the top of the sea; yet it is stated that they could not venture to take it in, as they were in very imminent danger and distress, the sea curling over the stern of the boat, and obliging them to bale with all their might.

The bread, being in bags, was in the greatest danger of being spoiled by the wet, the consequence of which, if not prevented, must have been fatal, as the whole party would inevitably be starved to death, if they should fortunately escape the fury of the waves. It was determined, therefore, that all superfluous clothes, with some rope and spare sails, should be thrown overboard, by which the boat was considerably lightened. The carpenter's tool-chest was cleared, and the tools stowed in the bottom of the boat, and the bread secured in the chest.

The sea continuing to run even higher than in the morning, the fatigue of bailing became very great; the boat was necessarily kept before the sea. The men were constantly wet, the night very cold, and at daylight their limbs were so benumbed that they could scarcely find the use of them. At this time a tea-spoonful of rum

C

was served out to each person. Five small cocoanuts were distributed for dinner, and every one was satisfied; and in the evening a few broken pieces of bread-fruit were served for supper, after which prayers were performed.

On the night of the 4th and morning of the 5th the gale had abated; the first step to be taken was to examine the state of the bread, a great part of which was found to be damaged and rotten—but even this was carefully preserved for use. The boat was now running among some islands, but after their reception at Tofoa, they did not venture to land. On the 6th they still continued to see islands at a distance; and this day, for the first time, they hooked a fish, to their great joy; "but," says the commander, "we were miserably disappointed by its being lost in trying to get it into the boat." In the evening each person had an ounce of the damaged bread, and a quarter of a pint of water for supper.

At dawn of day on the 7th, being very wet and cold, he says, "I served a spoonful of rum and a morsel of bread for breakfast."

In the course of this day they passed close to some rocky isles, from which two large sailing-canoes came swiftly after them, but in the afternoon gave over the chase. They were of the same construction as those of the Friendly Islands, and the land seen for the last two days was supposed to be the Fejee Islands. Heavy rain came on in the afternoon, when every person in the boat did his utmost to catch some water, and thus succeeded in increasing their stock to thirty-four gallons, besides quenching their thirst for the first time they had been able to do so since they had been at sea: but it seems an attendant consequence of the heavy rain caused them to pass the night very miserably; for being extremely wet, and having no dry things to shift or cover themselves, they experienced cold and shiverings scarcely to be conceived.

On the 8th, the allowance issued was an ounce and a half of pork, a tea-spoonful of rum, half a pint of cocoanut milk, and an ounce of bread. In the afternoon they were employed in cleaning out the boat, which occupied them until sunset before they got everything dry and in order. "Hitherto," Bligh says, "I had issued the allowance by guess, but I now made a pair of scales with two cocoanut shells; and having accidentally some pistol-balls in the boat, twenty-five of which weighed one pound, or sixteen ounces, I adopted one of these balls as the proportion of weight that each person should receive of bread at the times I served it. I also amused all hands with describing the situations of New-Guinea and New Holland, and gave them every information in my power, that in case any accident should happen to me, those who survived might have some idea of what they were about, and be able to find their way to Timor, which at present they knew nothing of more than the name, and some not even that. At night I served a quarter of a pint of water and half an ounce of bread for supper."

On the morning of the 9th, a quarter of a pint of cocoanut milk and some of the decayed bread were served for breakfast; and for dinner, the kernels of four cocoanuts, with the remainder of the rotten bread, which, he says, was eatable only by such distressed people as themselves. A storm of thunder and lightning gave them about twenty gallons of water.

The following day, the 10th, brought no relief, except that of its light. The sea broke over the boat so much, that two men were kept constantly bailing; and it was necessary to keep the boat before the waves for fear of its filling. The allowance now served regularly to each person was one twenty-fifth part of a pound of bread and a quarter of a pint of water, at eight in the morning, at noon, and at sunset. To-day was added about half an ounce of pork for dinner, which, though any moderate person would have considered it only as a mouthful, was divided into three or four.

The morning of the 11th did not improve. "At daybreak I served to each person a tea-spoonful of rum, our limbs being so much cramped that we could scarcely move them. Our situation was now extremely dangerous, the sea frequently running over our stern, which kept us bailing with all our strength. At noon the sun appeared, which gave us as much pleasure as is felt when it shows itself on a winter's day in England.

"In the evening of the 12th it still rained hard, and we again experienced a dreadful night. At length the day came, and showed a miserable set of beings, full of wants, without anything to relieve them. Some complained of great pain in their bowels, and every one of having almost lost the use of their limbs. The little sleep we got was in no way refreshing, as we were constantly covered with the sea and rain."

On the 13th and 14th the stormy weather and heavy sea continued unabated, and on these days they saw distant land, and passed several islands. The sight of these islands, it may well be supposed, served only to increase the misery of their situation. They were as men very little better than starving with plenty in their view; yet, to attempt procuring any relief was considered to be attended with so much danger, that the prolongation of life, even in the midst of misery, was thought preferable, while there remained hopes of being able to surmount their hardships.

The whole day and night of the 15th were still rainy; the latter was dark, not a star to be seen by which the steerage could be directed, and the sea was continually breaking over the boat. On the next day, the 16th, was issued for dinner an ounce of salt pork, in addition to their miserable allowance of one twenty-fifth part of a pound of bread. The night was again truly horrible, with storms of thunder, lightning, and rain; not a star visible, so that the steerage was quite uncertain.

Thus they continued with no abatement of their sufferings for another week, when Bligh thought it necessary to abridge the scanty allowance of bread; and, by agreement of the men, it was settled that every person should receive one twenty fifth part of a pound of bread for breakfast, and the same quantity for dinner, as usual, but that the proportion for supper should be discontinued; this arrangement left them forty-three days' consumption.

On the 25th about noon, some noddies came so near to the boat that one of them was caught by hand. This bird was about the size of a small pigeon. "I divided it," says Bligh, "with its entrails, into eighteen portions, and by a well-known method at sea, of '*Who shall have this?*' it was distributed, with the allowance of bread and water for dinner, and eaten up, bones and all, with salt water for sauce. In the evening, several boobies flying near to us, we had the good fortune to catch one of them. This bird is as large as a duck. They are the most presumptive proof of being near land of any sea-fowl we are acquainted with. I directed the bird to be killed for supper, and the blood to be given to three of the people who were the most distressed for want of food. The body, with the entrails, beak, and feet, I divided into eighteen shares, and with the allowance of bread, which I made a merit of granting, we made a good supper compared with our usual fare.

"On the next day, the 26th, we caught another booby, so that Providence appeared to be relieving our wants in an extraordinary manner. The people were overjoyed at this addition to their dinner, which was distributed in the same manner as on the preceding evening; giving the blood to those who were the most in want of food."

At one in the morning of the 28th, the person at the helm heard the sound of breakers. It was the "barrier reef" which runs along the eastern coast of New Holland, through which it now became the anxious object to discover a passage; Mr. Bligh says this was now become absolutely necessary, without a moment's loss of time. The idea of getting into smooth water and finding refreshments kept up the people's spirits. The sea broke furiously over the reef in every part; within, the water was so smooth and calm that every man already anticipated the heartfelt satisfaction he was about to receive, as soon as he should have passed the barrier. At length a break in the reef was discovered, a quarter of a mile in width, and through this the boat rapidly passed with a strong stream running to the westward, and came immediately into smooth water, and all the past hardships seemed at once to be forgotten.

They now returned thanks to God for his generous

4

protection, and with much content took their miserable allowance of the twenty-fifth part of a pound of bread and a quarter of a pint of water for dinner.

The coast now began to show itself very distinctly, and in the evening they landed on the sandy point of an island, when it was soon discovered there were oysters on the rocks, it being low water. The party sent out to reconnoitre returned highly rejoiced at having found plenty of oysters and fresh water. By help of a small magnifying glass a fire was made, and among the things that had been thrown into the boat was a tinderbox and a piece of brimstone, so that in future they had the ready means of making a fire. One of the men, too, had been so provident as to bring away with him from the ship a copper pot; and thus with a mixture of oysters, bread, and pork, a stew was made, of which each person received a full pint. It is remarked that the oysters grew so fast to the rocks, that it was with great difficulty they could be broken off; but they at length discovered it to be the most expeditious way to open them where they were fixed.

With oysters and palm-tops stewed together the people now made excellent meals, without consuming any of their bread. In the morning of the 30th Mr. Bligh saw with great delight a visible alteration in the men for the better, and he sent them away to gather oysters in order to carry a stock of them to sea, for he determined to put off again that evening. They also procured fresh water, and filled all their vessels to the amount of nearly sixty gallons. On examining the bread, it was found there still remained about thirty-eight days' allowance.

Being now ready for sea, every person was ordered to attend prayers; but just as they were embarking, about twenty naked savages made their appearance, running and hallooing, and beckoning the strangers to come to them; but as each was armed with a spear or lance, it was thought prudent to hold no communication with them. They now proceeded to the northward, having the continent on their left, and several islands and reefs on their right.

On the 31st they landed on one of these islands, to

which was given the name of "Sunday." On this island they obtained oysters, and clams, and dogfish; also a small bean, which Nelson, the botanist, pronounced to be a species of dolichos. On the 1st of June they stopped in the midst of some sandy islands, such as are known by the name of *keys*, where they procured a few clams and beans.

On the 3d of June, after passing several keys and islands, and doubling Cape York, the north-easternmost point of New Holland, at eight in the evening the little boat and her brave crew once more launched into the open ocean. "Miserable," says Lieutenant Bligh, "as our situation was in every respect, I was secretly surprised to see that it did not appear to affect any one so strongly as myself; on the contrary, it seemed as if they had embarked on a voyage to Timor in a vessel sufficiently calculated for safety and convenience. So much confidence gave me great pleasure, and I may venture to assert that to this cause our preservation is chiefly to be attributed. I encouraged every one with hopes that eight or ten days would bring us to a land of safety; and, after praying to God, for a continuance of his most gracious protection, I served out an allowance of water for supper, and directed our course to the west-south-west.

We had been just six days on the coast of New Holland, in the course of which we found oysters, a few clams, some birds, and water. But a benefit probably not less than this was that of being relieved from the fatigue of sitting constantly in the boat, and enjoying good rest at night. These advantages certainly preserved our lives; and small as the supply was, I am very sensible how much it alleviated our distresses. Before this time nature must have sunk under the extremes of hunger and fatigue. Even in our present situation, we were most deplorable objects, but the hopes of a speedy relief kept up our spirits. For my own part, incredible as it may appear, I felt neither extreme hunger nor thirst. My allowance contented me, knowing that I could have no more."

Another week of exposure in the open ocean greatly

reduced the strength of the sufferers. "In the morning of the 10th, after a very comfortless night, there was a visible alteration for the worse," says Mr. Bligh, "in many of the people, which gave me great apprehensions. An extreme weakness, swelled legs, hollow and ghastly countenances, a more than common inclination to sleep, with an apparent debility of understanding, seemed to me the melancholy presages of an approaching dissolution. The surgeon and Lebogue, in particular, were most miserable objects. I occasionally gave them a few tea-spoonfuls of wine out of the little that remained, which greatly assisted them. The hope of being able to accomplish the voyage was our principal support. The boatswain very innocently told me that he really thought I looked worse than any in the boat. The simplicity with which he uttered such an opinion amused me, and I returned him a better compliment."

On the 11th Lieutenant Bligh announced to his wretched companions that he had no doubt they had now passed the meridian of the eastern part of Timor, a piece of intelligence that diffused universal joy and satisfaction. Accordingly, at three in the morning of the following day, Timor was discovered at the distance only of two leagues from the shore.

"It is not possible for me," says this experienced navigator, "to describe the pleasure which the blessing of the sight of this land diffused among us. It appeared scarcely credible to ourselves, that, in an open boat, and so poorly provided, we should have been able to reach the coast of Timor in forty-one days after leaving Tofoa, having in that time run by our log a distance of three thousand six hundred and eighteen nautical miles; and that, notwithstanding our extreme distress, no one should have perished in the voyage."

On Sunday the 14th they came safely to anchor in Coupang Bay, where they were received with every mark of kindness, hospitality, and humanity. The houses of the principal people were thrown open for their reception. The poor sufferers, when landed, were scarcely able to walk; their condition is described as most deplorable. "The abilities of a painter could rarely, perhaps, have been displayed to more advantage than in the delineation of the two groups of figures which at this time presented themselves to each other. An indifferent spectator, if such could be found, would have been at a loss which most to admire, the eyes of famine sparkling at immediate relief, or the horror of their preservers at the sight of so many spectres, whose ghastly countenances, if the cause had been unknown, would rather have excited terror than pity. Our bodies were nothing but skin and bones, our limbs were full of sores, and we were clothed in rags; in this condition, with the tears of joy and gratitude flowing down our cheeks, the people of Timor beheld us with a mixture of horror, surprise, and pity.

"When," continues the commander, "I reflect how providentially our lives were saved at Tofoa, by the Indians delaying their attack; and that, with scarcely anything to support life, we crossed a sea of more than twelve hundred leagues, without shelter from the inclemency of the weather; when I reflect that in an open boat, with so much stormy weather, we escaped foundering, that not any of us were taken off by disease, that we had the great good fortune to pass the unfriendly natives of other countries without accident, and at last to meet with the most friendly and best of people to relieve our distresses—I say, when I reflect on all these wonderful escapes, the remembrance of such great mercies enables me to bear with resignation and cheerfulness the failure of an expedition, the success of which I had so much at heart, and which was frustrated at a time when I was congratulating myself on the fairest prospect of being able to complete it in a manner that would fully have answered the intention of his majesty and the humane promoters of so benevolent a plan."

Having recruited their strength by a residence of two months among the friendly inhabitants of Coupang, they proceeded to the westward on the 20th August in a small schooner, which was purchased and armed for the purpose, and arrived on the 1st October in Batavia Road, where Mr. Bligh embarked in a Dutch packet, and was landed on the Isle of Wight on the 14th of March, 1790.

4*

The rest of the people had passages provided for them in ships of the Dutch East India Company, then about to sail for Europe; but, as before mentioned, only twelve of them survived to reach England.

Thus ended a voyage of the most extraordinary nature that ever happened; and it is impossible to read it without giving praise to the discretion, skill, and energy, displayed by the commander. He had not only to combat the dangers of the sea in an open boat, but to contend with the ignorance and caprice of men, who were near perishing with hunger, yet often tantalized with the appearance of land, clothed with verdure, which they could not approach, through fear that the natives might destroy them. And what required the highest degree of wisdom and firmness was a rigid adherence to the compact respecting their daily allowance of food, when the provisions were all within their reach, and could be seized at any moment. Nor was it a less task to prevent despondency from taking entire possession of their minds, for which purpose he must contrive to divert their attention; to accomplish which, a log-line was prepared, and hourly hove, and the men were practised in counting seconds correctly, so as to ascertain the distance run on each day; and often when the sun was out, and at night when the stars appeared, Lieutenant Bligh took observations for finding their latitude. When the party were a little recruited by their temporary rest of six days among the coral islands off the coast of New Holland, a new demand was made for prompt and decisive action in the commander, to meet properly a rising tumult and mutiny, which, if not checked at the moment, must have ended in the inevitable ruin of the whole company.

The reader is perhaps impatient to learn what became of the men who mutinied on board the ship Bounty, and took her from the hands of the commander. The next chapter will give the information in part.

CHAPTER V.

THE SEARCH.

"* * * 'Where lurk the mutineers meanwhile?
Or whither roam those miscreants vile?
Search every island, traverse every shore,
The hills and wilds and caverns dark explore;
The guilty from his den let justice draw,
To feel the majesty of British law.'
Thus cried the mass; and in th' indignant sound
Each note of mercy's milder voice was drown'd."

AFTER the return of Lieutenant Bligh, the people in England, filled with indignation against Christian and his associates, expressed a strong desire that they might be found and brought to justice, and the government sent out the ship Pandora, under Captain Edwards, to search for the Bounty and the mutineers that seized her, in order that the men might be brought to trial and punished according to the laws of the country. The Pandora sailed immediately to Tahiti, and anchored in Matavai Bay on the 23d of March, 1791.

Let us now return to the day of the mutiny, April 28, 1789. After forcing Bligh into the launch, the mutineers sailed for Tahiti, as he supposed they would, although, for the purpose of deceiving him, they at first steered in a different direction. In a few days they found some difficulty in reaching that island, and bore away for Toobouai, in latitude 20° 13′ south, and longitude 149° 35′ west, where they anchored on the 25th of May. They had thrown overboard the greater part of the bread-fruit plants, and divided among themselves the property of the officers and men who had been so inhumanly turned adrift. At this island they intended to form a settlement, but the opposition of the natives, the want of many necessary materials, and quarrels among themselves, determined them to go to Tahiti to procure what might be required to effect their purpose provided they should agree to prosecute their original intention. They accordingly sailed from Toobouai about the latter end of the month, and arrived at Tahiti on the 6th June. The otoo, or reigning sovereign, and other principal natives, were very inquisitive and anxious to know what had become of Lieutenant Bligh and the rest of the crew, and also what had been done with the bread-fruit plants. They were told they had most unexpectedly fallen in with Captain Cook, at an island he had just discovered, called Whytootakee, where he intended to form a settlement, and where the plants had been landed; and that Lieutenant Bligh and the others were stopping there to assist Captain Cook in the business he had in hand, and that he had appointed Mr. Christian commander of the Bounty; and that he was now come by his orders for an additional supply of hogs, goats, fowls, bread-fruit, and various other articles which Tahiti could supply.

This artful story was quite sufficient to impose on the credulity of these humane and simple-minded islanders; and so overcome with joy were they to hear that their old friend Captain Cook was alive, and about to settle so near them, that every possible means were forthwith made use of to procure the things that were wanted; so that in the course of a very few days the Bounty received on board three hundred and twelve hogs, thirty-eight goats, eight dozen of fowls, a bull and a cow, and a large quantity of bread-fruit, plantains, bananas, and other fruits. They also took with them eight men, nine women, and seven boys. With these supplies they left Tahiti on the 19th June, and arrived a second time at Toobouai on the 26th. They warped the ship up the harbor, landed the live stock, and set about building a fort of fifty yards square.

While this work was carrying on, quarrels and disagreements were daily happening among them, and continual disputes and skirmishes were taking place with the natives, generally brought on by the violent conduct of the invaders, and by depredations committed on their property. Retaliations were attempted by the natives without success, numbers of whom, being pursued with firearms were put to death. Still the situation of the mutineers became so disagreeable and unsafe, the work went on so slowly and reluctantly, that the building of the fort was agreed to be discontinued. Christian, in fact, had very soon perceived that his authority was on the wane, and that no peaceful establishment was likely to be accomplished at Toobouai; he therefore held a consultation as to what would be the most advisable step to take. After much angry discussion, it was at length determined that Toobouai should be abandoned; that the ship should once more be taken to Tahiti; and that those who might choose to go on shore there might do so, and those who preferred to remain in the ship might proceed in her to whatever place they should agree upon among themselves.

In consequence of this determination, they sailed from Toobouai on the 15th, and arrived at Matavai Bay on the 20th September, 1789. Here sixteen of the mutineers were put on shore, at their own request; because they preferred to remain at Tahiti instead of following Christian to make a settlement on some other island. The remaining nine agreed to continue in the Bounty. The small arms, powder, canvass, and the small stores belonging to the ship were equally divided among the whole crew. The Bounty sailed finally from Tahiti on the night of the 21st September, and was last seen the following morning to the north-west of Point Venus. They took with them seven Tahitian men and twelve women. It was not even conjectured whither they meant to go; but Christian had frequently been heard to say, that his object was to discover some unknown or uninhabited island, in which there was no harbor for shipping; that he would run the Bounty on shore, and make use of her materials to form a settlement.

Nothing more was known at Tahiti respecting Christian and the party with him in the Bounty, when Captain Edwards arrived. On the very day of his arrival, three of the sixteen pirates or mutineers left behind by the Bounty, went voluntarily on board the Pandora, but were immediately put in irons. These were, Coleman, the armorer, and Peter Heywood and George Stewart midshipmen. Four others were soon found and confined. Two of the most active in the mutiny, Churchill and Thompson, had perished by violent death some time before the arrival of the Pandora; they had both accompanied a distinguished chief, who, dying without children, left his property and office to Churchill; after which, Thompson, for some real or fancied insult, took an opportunity to shoot his companion: the natives assembled to avenge this outrage, and literally stoned the murderer to death. Thompson's skull was brought on board the Pandora. The remaining six of the pirates had, on the day before Captain Edwards arrived, sailed out from Matavai Bay in a small schooner which they had built; on learning which, he immediately sent two Lieutenants with the pinnace and launch to intercept the vessel. They soon got sight of her and chased her out to sea; but the schooner gained upon them, and, night coming on, they gave up the pursuit. This schooner had been constructed by the advice and help of Morrison, who considered himself innocent as to the mutiny, and whose object was to reach Batavia, and thence find a passage to England. But after being chased by the lieutenants from the Pandora, the schooner returned to Tahiti for some reason, probably because they had not obtained a sufficient supply of necessaries for a voyage; and the lieutenants were again sent out by Captain Edwards; and the schooner was found at Papane and taken: but the mutineers had fled to the mountains; shortly after, however, they were found, and, surrendering themselves, were brought as prisoners to the ship.

The fourteen men thus secured were kept in irons in a kind of round-house, which was small, and was entered by a scuttle in the roof, about eighteen inches square. This was called "Pandora's Box." Some of the prisoners were said to be married to the daughters of the most respectable chiefs, on which account the natives were greatly distressed at the idea of their being confined as criminals. Their wives visited the ship and brought their children. "To see the poor captives in irons," said an eye-witness, "weeping over their tender offspring, was too moving a scene for any feeling heart. Their wives brought them ample supplies of every delicacy that the country afforded while we lay there, and behaved with the greatest fidelity and affection to them." Of the strength of their attachment a very striking instance was afforded in the case of the wife of George Stewart, the daughter of a chief, of great landed property, near Matavai Bay; her story is told in the account of the missionaries who were sent to Tahiti, as I have before mentioned, about the year 1797. "The history of Peggy Stewart marks a tenderness of heart that never will be heard without emotion: she was daughter of a chief, and taken for his wife by Mr. Stewart, one of the unhappy mutineers. They had lived with the old chief in the most tender state of endearment; a beautiful little girl had been the fruit of their union, and was at the breast when the Pandora arrived, seized the criminals, and secured them in irons on board the ship. Frantic with grief, the unhappy Peggy (for so he had named her) flew with her infant in a canoe to the arms of her husband. The interview was so affecting and afflicting, that the officers on board were overwhelmed with anguish, and Stewart himself, unable to bear the heart-rending scene, begged she might not be admitted again on board. She was separated from him by violence, and conveyed on shore in a state of despair and grief too big for utterance. Withheld from him, and forbidden to come any more on board, she sunk into the deepest dejection; it preyed on her vitals; she lost all relish for food and life, rejoiced no more, pined under a rapid decay of two months, and fell a victim to her feelings, dying literally of a broken heart. Her child is yet alive, and the tender object of our care, having been brought up by a sister, who nursed it as her own, and has discharged all the duties of an affectionate mother to the orphan infant."

Fourteen of the mutineers were now in close and safe custody; but where were the rest, and their ringleader Christian? On the 8th of May, Captain Edwards left Tahiti to search for them, having no clew to guide him except the vague information that Christian had expressed an intention to retire to some uninhabited island.

The captain visited many islands, among which were several not at that time designated upon any map or chart; but nothing was learned respecting the pirates or their vessel, except that on one island a sailor picked up a sail-yard, which had the name of the Bounty marked upon it. After a fruitless search for three months, the Pandora arrived, on the 28th of August, 1791, on the coast of New Holland, and close to that extraordinary reef of coral rocks called the "Barrier Reef," which runs along the greater part of the eastern coast, but at a considerable distance from it. Upon this reef, unhappily, in the course of the night, the vessel struck, and immediately began to let in water; all hands were turned to pumping and bailing: by the greatest efforts the ship was kept from sinking through the night; but early in the morning of the 29th, she went down so suddenly that thirty-five persons on board were buried with her in the sea. The others "had just time to leap overboard, accompanying it with a dreadful yell. The cries of the men drowning in the water were at first awful in the extreme; but as they sunk and became faint, they died away by degrees."

"She gave a heel, and then a lurch to port,
And, going down head foremost—sunk. * * * *

Then rose from sea to sky the wild farewell!
Then shriek'd the timid and stood still the brave;
Then some leap'd overboard with dreadful yell,
As eager to anticipate their grave;
And the sea yawn'd around her like a hell,
And down she suck'd with her the whirling wave,
Like one who grapples with his enemy,
And strives to strangle him before he die.

And first one universal shriek there rush'd
Louder than the loud ocean, like a crash
Of echoing thunder; and then all was hush'd,
Save the wild wind and the remorseless dash
Of billows; but at intervals there gush'd
Accompanied with a convulsive splash,
A solitary shriek—the bubbling cry
Of some strong swimmer in his agony."

After daylight appeared, the officers thought nothing more could be done to save the ship: "it then became necessary," says Captain Edwards, in his account of the disaster, "to endeavor to provide means for the preservation of the people. Our four boats, which consisted of one launch, one eight-oared pinnace, and two six-oared yawls, with careful hands in them, were kept astern of the ship; a small quantity of bread, water, and other necessary articles, were put into them; two canoes which we had on board were lashed together and put into the water; rafts were made, and all floating things upon deck were unlashed.

"About half-past six in the morning of the 29th the hold was full, and the water was between decks, and it also washed in at the upper deck ports, and there were strong indications that the ship was on the very point of sinking, and we began to leap overboard and take to the boats, and before everybody could get out of her she actually sunk. The boats continued astern of the ship in the direction of the drift of the tide from her, and took up the people that had hold of rafts and other floating things that had been cast loose, for the purpose of supporting them on the water. The double canoe, that was able to support a considerable number of men, broke adrift with only one man, and was bulged upon a reef, and afforded us no assistance when she was so much wanted on this trying and melancholy occasion. Two of the boats were laden with men, and sent to a small sandy island (or key) about four miles from the wreck; and I remained near the ship for some time with the other two boats, and picked up all the people that could be seen, and then followed the first two boats to the key; and having landed the men and cleared the boats, they were immediately despatched again to look about the wreck and the adjoining reef for any that might be missing, but they returned without having found a single person. On mustering the people that were saved, it appeared that eighty-nine of the ship's company, and ten of the mutineers that had been prisoners on board, answered to their names; but thirty-one of the ship's company, and four mutineers, were lost with the ship.' The melancholy scene described above is partially represented in the engraving on page 51.

But how did any of the mutineers escape being sunk

with the ship? Did Captain Edwards, actuated by feelings of humanity, free them from their irons, and allow them to save themselves if they could? He certainly did not act thus humanely at first; for in the night, three of them were let out of irons and sent to work at the pumps, while two sentinels were placed over the others, although they begged to be permitted to help in saving the ship and their own lives. Whether the captain afterwards took any notice of them appears to be uncertain; and it is not known whether it was by accident or by design that the master-at-arms let the keys of their irons fall through the scuttle, and thus enabled them to commence their own liberation, in which they were assisted by William Moulter, a boatswain's mate, at the hazard of being drowned himself; he pulled the bars through the shackles, saying he would set them free, or go to the bottom with them.

Captain Edwards, in his narrative, says very little respecting his prisoners, from the day in which they were consigned to "Pandora's Box." He seems to have considered it his duty to hold them in the strictest confinement, and never allow his feelings to be disturbed by their sufferings. Whatever may have been the necessity or the expediency of keeping them in irons from day to day, without the benefit of fresh air and exercise, there was neither necessity nor common humanity in leaving them in fetters when the ship was every moment liable to sink; when, if any of them might be disposed to escape from justice, it would be next to impossible to do it; and when some of them (among whom was particularly George Stewart) desired to reach home and throw themselves on God and their country as innocent men.

On the sandy key which fortunately presented itself the shipwrecked seamen hauled up the boats, to repair those that were damaged, and to stretch canvass round the gunwales, the better to keep out the sea from breaking into them. The heat of the sun and the reflection from the sand are described as excruciating, and the thirst of the men was rendered intolerable, from their stomachs being filled with salt-water in the length of

Wreck of the Pandora.

time they had to swim before being picked up. Dr. Hamilton says, they were greatly disturbed in the night by the irregular behavior of one of the seamen, named Connell, which made them suspect he had got drunk with some wine that had been saved; but it turned out that the excruciating torture he suffered from thirst had induced him to drink salt water; "by which means he went mad, and died in the sequel of the voyage." It seems, a small keg of water and some biscuits had been thrown into one of the boats, which they found, by calculation, would be sufficient to last sixteen days, on an allowance of two wineglasses of water per day to each man, and a very small quantity of bread, the weight of which was accurately ascertained by a musket-ball and a pair of wooden scales made for each boat.

The crew and the prisoners were now distributed among the four boats. At Bligh's "Mountainous Island" they entered a bay where swarms of natives came down and made signs for their landing; but this they declined to do; on which an arrow was discharged and struck one of the boats; and as the savages were seen to be collecting their bows and arrows, a volley of muskets, a few of which happened to be in the boats, was discharged, which put them to flight. While sailing among the islands and near the shore, they now and then stopped to pick up a few oysters and procure a little fresh water. On the 2d September they passed the north-west point of New Holland, and launched into the great Indian Ocean, having a voyage of about a thousand miles still to perform.

It will be recollected that Captain Bligh's people received warmth and comfort by wringing out their clothes in salt-water. The same practice was adopted by the crews of the Pandora's boats; but Dr. Hamilton observes, that "this wetting their bodies with salt water is not advisable, if protracted beyond three or four days, as after that time the great absorption from the skin that takes place taints the fluids with the bitter part of salt water, so that the saliva becomes intolerable in the mouth." Their mouths, indeed, he says, became so parched, that few attempted to eat the slender allowance of bread. He also remarks, that as the sufferings of the people continued, their temper became cross and savage. In the captain's boat, it is stated, one of the mutineers took to praying; but that "the captain, suspecting the purity of his doctrines, and unwilling that he should have a monopoly of the business, gave prayers himself."

On the 13th they saw the Island of Timor, and the next morning landed and got some water and a few small fish from the natives; and on the night of the 15th anchored opposite the fort of Coupang. Nothing could exceed the kindness and hospitality of the governor and other Dutch officers of this settlement, in affording every possible assistance and relief to their distressed condition. At length, they obtained means of returning to England, where Captain Edwards arrived with his ten prisoners on the 19th of June, 1792.

And how were the prisoners treated on being brought to England? A court-martial to try them was immediately ordered, and assembled for the purpose on board his Majesty's ship Duke, on the 12th of September, and continued its sittings until the 18th of the same month, Vice Admiral Lord Hood being the president of the court. The evidence presented to the court consisted of the narrative furnished by Lieutenant Bligh, and the testimony of several of the men who were put with him into the launch, and that of Captain Edwards. Four of the prisoners were acquitted as not guilty, as there was no evidence that they participated in the mutiny, and especially as they were mentioned in Bligh's narrative as having been detained on board the Bounty against their will. The other six were condemned, and sentenced to suffer death by being hanged by the neck on board of some ship of war; two of them, however, James Morrison and Peter Heywood, were earnestly recommended to his majesty's mercy. On the 24th of October the king's warrant was issued, granting a full pardon to Morrison and Heywood, and a respite to William Muspratt, who was afterwards also pardoned, but ordering the execution of the other three, which took place on the 29th of the month, on board his majesty's ship

5*

Brunswick, in Portsmouth harbor. While all persons who were acquainted with the facts, agreed that the sentence of the court as to the three that were finally executed was perfectly just, there were many who felt differently in respect to the three others, and especially in respect to Peter Heywood. It should be remembered, however, that the court were not at liberty to pass any sentence except death or a full acquittal; that the crimes of mutiny and piracy deserve the punishment of death as truly as murder and highway robbery; and that the mere circumstance that these prisoners remained with the mutineers must be evidence against them, unless it could be shown that they were detained contrary to their choice, by Christian and his party.

The case of Peter Heywood is particularly interesting, on account, not only of his real character and subsequent life, but also of the distress and anxiety felt by his widowed mother and affectionate sister, from the time of Bligh's return, in March, 1790, until the promulgation of the king's warrant, in October, 1792. But this must form the subject of another chapter.

CHAPTER VI.

THE HEYWOODS.

"Oh, fatal voyage! which robb'd my soul of peace
And wrecked my happiness in stormy seas!
Why, my lov'd Lycidas, why didst thou stay?
Why waste thy life from friendship far away?
* * * * * * *
Indulgent Heaven, in pity to our tears,
At length will bless a parent's sinking years;
Again shall I behold thy lovely face,
By manhood form'd, and ripen'd ev'ry grace;
Again I'll press thee to my anxious breast,
And every sorrow shall be hush'd to rest."

NESSY.

It is worthy of notice, that the chief evidence offered against Heywood came from Thomas Hayward and John Hallet, who were midshipmen in the Bounty, and, having returned with Bligh, had been promoted, and at the time of the trial held each the rank of lieutenant. It is also worthy of notice, that a manuscript journal kept by Morrison on board the Bounty was some how preserved by him through his stay with Christian and at Tahiti, and even through the wreck of the Pandora, and found among the papers left by Peter Heywood. This journal agrees with other documents in respect of dates, and is of undoubted genuineness, and there is no ground to question its authenticity. Morrison, it may here be remarked, was a person of talent and education above the situation he held in the Bounty, that of boatswain's mate ; he had previously served in the navy as midshipman, and after his pardon above mentioned, he was appointed gunner of the Blenheim, in which he perished with Sir Thomas Trowbridge, the vessel being lost in a storm in 1807.

Now it appears, from this journal, as before quoted on page 28, that Hayward and Hallet were the mates of the third watch, on the fatal morning of the mutiny, and were asleep when they should have been at the post of duty, and that it was this very circumstance which suggested to Christian the first idea of seizing the ship, and also at the same time furnished him with an opportunity to do it. Had these facts been known to Lieutenant Bligh, and his mind not been wholly misled under the false imagination of a preconcerted conspiracy, these two midshipmen, on reaching England, would have probably been dismissed from service instead of being promoted. Had Hayward and Hallet known that the tumult which burst upon them when they were scarcely awaked from sleep, was not the result of a premeditated plan, it is probable that they would not have been so ready as they were to consider Heywood implicated in the mutiny ; they do not appear to have shown any more forwardness at the time to help the commander than Heywood did ; they were young, Hallet being only about fifteen years of age, and were both alarmed, as was testified in court. It is not surprising that they were thrown into a confusion of mind which hindered their acting as they otherwise would, and also hindered their remembering perfectly what transpired. But, after all, there was nothing in the testimony given respecting Heywood, that could have led to his condemnation, had Lieutenant Bligh's narrative only contained a statement that he was detained in the Bounty by force, as it did respecting some others. It has been ascertained, that in this narrative presented to the court there is an omission of several passages which are contained in his original manuscript journal. One of these passages is the following: "as for the officers whose cabins were in the cock-pit, there was no relief for them; they endeavored to come to my assistance, but were not allowed to put their heads above the hatchway;" this passage was applicable to Peter Heywood and George Stewart only, who were in fact kept below by order of the mutineer, Churchill, he knowing that they were intending to go into the boat. Heywood feared very much to go into the boat, as it seemed to him inevitable death; but on being reminded by Stewart (as he always thought, although Hayward said in court that it was himself who reminded him) that he would be deemed guilty if he remained in the ship, went immediately below intending to get some things and go into the boat. One of the witnesses testified in court that he saw Heywood go below, and supposed it was his intention to follow the party in the boat; and that, after this, when Heywood and Stewart were below, he heard Churchill cry out, "Keep them below." Such being the circumstances, no one can help feeling that Lieutenant Bligh acted with great unfairness in suppressing the passage above cited. There can scarcely be a doubt that it was originally written under a correct impression made upon his mind by his own observation; to suppose he suppressed it by deliberate malice is too serious a charge; he did it, probably, because his original impressions were subsequently altered by conversation with Hallet and Hayward; but by so doing he unjustly inflicted a stigma upon Stewart, who perished in the melancholy wreck of the Pandora, and occasioned the condemnation of Heywood; the innocence of both of whom is confirmed by the fact, that they hastened voluntarily on board the Pandora, as soon as she arrived at Tahiti.

Peter Heywood was born in the Isle of Man; his father being deemster of Man, and seneschal to the Duke of Athol. In 1787 he left his home, to sail as midshipman in the Bounty, under fifteen years of age, a boy admired and beloved by all who knew him, and to his own family almost an object of adoration, for his superior understanding and the amiable qualities of his disposition. His deportment at sea, before the mutiny, appears to have been such as might have been expected from such a boy; as every witness in court testified highly in his favor when the question was asked respecting his conduct and temper on board the ship; the answers were, "Beloved by everybody;" "Always a very good character;" "The most amiable and deserving of every one's esteem;" "In every respect becoming a gentleman, and such as merited the esteem of everybody." Up to the moment when the Bounty sailed out of sight of her rightful commander, Lieutenant Bligh seems to have cherished towards him sentiments in perfect harmony with these strong expressions; and it is difficult to explain the unfeeling manner in which that officer replied to the anxious inquiries made on his return to England by young Heywood's mother. This affectionate woman, deeply afflicted by the recent death of her husband, and distracted by a report that her son was one of the ring-leaders in the mutiny, and that he even went with them armed into the captain's cabin, addressed to Bligh a letter written in all a mother's tenderness. The following is his reply:—

"*London, April 2d,* 1790.

"MADAM,

"I received your letter this day, and feel for you very much, being perfectly sensible of the extreme distress you must suffer from the conduct of your son Peter. *His baseness is beyond all description;* but I hope you will endeavor to prevent the loss of him, heavy as the misfortune is, from afflicting you too severely. I imagine he is, with the rest of the mutineers returned to Tahiti. I am, madam,

(Signed) "WM. BLIGH."

Colonel Holwell, the uncle of young Heywood, had previously addressed Bligh on the same melancholy subject, to whom he returned the following answer:—

"26th *March*, 1790.

"Sir,

"I have just this instant received your letter. With much concern I inform you that your nephew, Peter Heywood, is among the mutineers. *His ingratitude to me is of the blackest dye*, for I was a father to him in every respect, and he never once had an angry word from me through the whole course of the voyage, as his conduct always gave me much pleasure and satisfaction. I very much regret *that so much baseness formed the character of a young man* I had a real regard for, and it will give me much pleasure to hear that his friends *can bear the loss of him without much concern.* I am, sir, &c.

(Signed) "Wm. Bligh."

As a contrast to these ungracious letters, it is a great relief to peruse the correspondence that took place between this unfortunate young officer and his amiable but dreadfully afflicted family. The letters of his sister Nessy Heywood (of which a few will be inserted in the course of this narrative) exhibit so lively and ardent an affection for her beloved brother, are couched in so high a tone of feeling for his honor and confidence in his innocence, and are so nobly answered by the suffering youth, that no apology seems to be required for their introduction.

The following letter of Heywood to his mother removes all doubt as to the character and conduct of this officer. It is an artless and pathetic tale, and, as his sister says, "breathes not a syllable inconsistent with truth and honor."

"*Batavia, November* 20*th*, 1791.

"My ever-honored and dearest Mother,

"At length the time has arrived when you are once more to hear from your ill-fated son, whose conduct at the capture of that ship in which it was my fortune to embark has, I fear, from what has since happened to me, been grossly misrepresented to you by Lieutenant Bligh, who, by not knowing the real cause of my remaining on board, naturally suspected me, unhappily for me, to be a coadjutor in the mutiny; but I never, to my knowledge, while under his command, behaved myself in a manner unbecoming the station I occupied, nor so much as even entertained a thought derogatory to his honor, so as to give him the least grounds for entertaining an opinion of me so ungenerous and undeserved; for I flatter myself he cannot give a character of my conduct, while I was under his tuition, that could merit the slightest reproach. Oh! my dearest mother, I hope you have not so easily credited such an account of me; do but let me vindicate my conduct, and declare to you the true cause of my remaining in the ship, and you will then see how little I deserve censure, and how I have been injured by so gross an aspersion. I shall then give you a short and cursory account of what has happened to me since; but I am afraid to say a hundredth part of what I have got in store, for I am not allowed the use of writing materials, if known, so that this is done by stealth; but if it should ever come to your hands, it will, I hope, have the desired effect of removing your uneasiness on my account, when I assure you, before the face of God, of my innocence of what is laid to my charge. How I came to remain on board was thus:—

"The morning the ship was taken, it being my watch below, happening to awake just after daylight, and looking out of my hammock, I saw a man sitting upon the arm chest in the main hatchway, with a drawn cutlass in his hand, the reason of which I could not divine; so I got out of bed and inquired of him what was the cause of it. He told me that Mr. Christian, assisted by some of the ship's company, had seized the captain and put him in confinement; had taken the command of the ship, and meant to carry Bligh home a prisoner, in order to try him by court-martial for his long tyrannical and oppressive conduct to his people. I was quite thunderstruck; and hurrying into my berth again, told one of my messmates, whom I awakened out of his sleep, what had happened. Then dressing myself, I went up the fore-hatchway, and saw what he had told me was but too true; and again I asked some of the people who were under arms what was going to be done with the captain, who was then on the larboard side of the quarter-deck, with his hands tied behind his back, and Mr. Christian alongside him with a pistol and drawn bayonet. I now heard a very different story, and that the captain was to be sent ashore to Tofoa in the launch, and that those who would not join Mr. Christian might either accompany the captain, or would be taken in irons to Tahiti and left there. The relation of two stories so different left me unable to judge which could be the true one; but seeing them hoisting the boats out, it seemed to prove the latter.

"In this trying situation, young and inexperienced as I was, and without an adviser (every person being, as it were, infatuated, and not knowing what to do), I remained for a while a silent spectator of what was going on; and after revolving the matter in my mind, I determined to choose what I thought the less of two evils, and stay by the ship; for I had no doubt that those who went on shore in the launch would be put to death by the savage natives, whereas the Tahitians being a humane and generous race, one might have a hope of being kindly received, and remain there until the arrival of some ship, which seemed, to silly me, the most consistent with reason and rectitude.

"While this resolution possessed my mind, at the same time lending my assistance to hoist out the boats, the hurry and confusion affairs were in, and thinking my intention just, I never thought of going to Mr. Bligh for advice; besides, what confirmed me in it was, my seeing two experienced officers, when ordered into the boat by Mr. Christian, desire his permission to remain in the ship; one of whom my own messmate (Mr. Hayward,) and I being assisting to clear the launch of yams, he asked me what I intended to do; I told him, to remain in the ship. Now, this answer, I imagine, he has told Mr. Bligh I made to him; from which, together with my not speaking to him that morning, his suspicions of me have arisen, construing my conduct into what is foreign to my nature.

"Thus, my dearest mother, it was all owing to my youth and unadvised inexperience, but has been interpreted into villany and disregard of my country's laws, the ill effects of which I at present, and still am to labor under for some months longer. And now, after what I have asserted, I may still once more retrieve my injured reputation, be again reinstated in the affection and favor of the most tender of mothers, and be still considered as her ever dutiful son.

"I was not undeceived in my erroneous decision till too late, which was after the captain was in the launch; for while I was talking to the master-at-arms, one of the ringleaders in the affair, my other messmate, whom I had left in his hammock in the berth (Mr. Stewart) came up to me, and asked me if I was not going in the launch. I replied, No; upon which he told me not to think of such a thing as remaining behind, but take his advice, and go down below with him to get a few necessary things, and make haste to go with him into the launch; adding, that by remaining in the ship I should incur an equal share of guilt with the mutineers themselves. I reluctantly followed his advice—I say *reluctantly*, because I knew no better, and was foolish; and the boat swimming very deep in the water—the land being far distant—the thoughts of being sacrificed by the natives—and the self-consciousness of my first intention being just—all these considerations almost staggered my resolution; however, I preferred my companion's judgment to my own, and we both jumped down the main-hatchway to prepare ourselves for the boat—but no sooner were we in the berth, than the master-at-arms ordered the sentry to keep us both in the berth till he should receive orders to release us. We desired the master-at-arms to acquaint Mr. Bligh of our intention, which we had reason to think he never did, nor were we permitted to come on deck until the launch was a long way astern. I now, when too late, saw my error.

"At the latter end of May, we got to an island to the southward of Tahiti, called Tooboui, where they intended to make a settlement, but finding no stock there of any kind, they agreed to go to Tahiti, and, after procuring hogs and fowls, to return to Tooboui and remain. So, on the 6th June we arrived at Tahiti, where I was in hopes I might find an opportunity of running away, and remaining on shore, but I could not effect it, as there was always too good a look-out kept to prevent any such steps being taken. And besides they had all sworn that should any one make his escape, they would force the natives to restore him, and would then shoot him as an example to the rest; well knowing, that any one, by remaining there, might be the means (should a ship arrive) of discovering their intended place of abode. Finding it, therefore, impracticable, I saw no other alternative but to rest as content as possible and return to Tooboui, and there wait till the masts of the Bounty should be taken out, and then take the boat which might carry me to Tahiti, and disable those remaining from pursuit. But Providence so ordered it, that we had no occasion to try our fortune at such a hazard, for, upon returning there and remaining till the latter end of August, in which time a fort was almost built, but nothing could be effected; and as the natives could not be brought to friendly terms, and with whom we had many skirmishes, and narrow escapes from being cut off by them, and what was still worse, internal broils and discontent,—these things determined part of the people to leave the island and go to Tahiti, which was carried by a majority of votes.

"This being carried into execution on the 20th September, and having anchored in Matavai Bay, the next morning my messmate (Mr. Stewart) and I went on shore, to the house of an old landed proprietor, our former friend; and being now set free from a lawless crew, determined to remain as much apart from them as possible, and wait patiently for the arrival of a ship. Fourteen more of the Bounty's people came likewise on shore, and Mr. Christian and eight men went away with the ship, but God knows whither. While we remained here, we were treated by our kind and friendly natives with a generosity and humanity almost unparalleled, and such as we could hardly have expected from the most civilized people.

"To be brief—having remained here till the latter end of March, 1791, on the 26th of that month his Majesty's ship Pandora arrived, and had scarcely anchored, when my messmate and I went on board and made ourselves known; and having learned from one of the natives who had been off in a canoe, that our former messmate Mr. Hayward, now promoted to the rank of a lieutenant, was on board, we asked for him,

6

supposing he might prove the assertions of our innocence. But he (like all worldings when raised a little in life) received us very coolly, and pretended ignorance of our affairs; yet formerly, he and I were bound in brotherly love and friendship. Appearances being so much against us, we were ordered to be put in irons, and looked upon—oh, infernal words!—as *piratical villains.* A rebuff so severe as this was, to a person unused to troubles, would perhaps have been insupportable; but to me, who had now been long inured to the frowns of fortune, and feeling myself supported by an inward consciousness of not deserving it, it was received with the greatest composure, and a full determination to bear it with patience.

"My sufferings, however, I have not power to describe; but though they are great, yet I thank God for enabling me to bear them without repining. I endeavor to qualify my affliction with these three considerations: first, my innocence not deserving them; secondly, that they cannot last long: and thirdly, that the change may be for the better. The first improves my hopes, the second my patience, and the third my courage. I am young in years, but old in what the world calls adversity; and it has had such an effect, as to make me consider it the most beneficial incident that could have occurred at my age. It has made me acquainted with three things which are little known, and as little believed by any but those who have felt their effects: first, the villany and censoriousness of mankind; secondly, the futility of all human hopes; and thirdly, the happiness of being content in whatever station it may please Providence to place me. In short, it has made me more of a philosopher, than many years of a life spent in ease and pleasure would have done.

"As they will, no doubt, proceed to the greatest lengths against me, I being the only surviving officer, and they most inclined to believe a prior story, all that can be said to confute it will probably be looked upon as mere falsity and invention. Should that be my unhappy case, and they resolved upon my destruction as an example to futurity, may God enable me to bear my fate with the fortitude of a man, conscious that misfortune, not any misconduct, is the cause, and that the Almighty can attest my innocence. Yet why should I despond? I have, I hope, still a friend in that Providence which hath preserved me amid many greater dangers, and upon whom alone I now depend for safety. God will always protect those who deserve it. These are the sole considerations which have enabled me to make myself easy and content under my past misfortunes.

"Twelve more of the people who were at Tahiti having delivered themselves up, there was a sort of prison built on the after-part of the quarter-deck, into which we were all put in close confinement, with both legs and both hands in irons, and were treated with great rigor, not being allowed ever to get out of this den; and being obliged to eat, drink, sleep, and obey the calls of nature here, you may form some idea of the disagreeable situation I must have been in, unable as I was to help myself (being deprived of the use of both my legs and hands), but by no means adequate to the reality.

"On the 9th May we left Tahiti, and proceeded to the Friendly Islands, and about the beginning of August got in among the reefs of New Holland, to endeavor to discover a passage through them; but it was not effected, for the Pandora, ever unlucky, and as if devoted by Heaven to destruction, was driven by a current upon the patch of a reef, and on which, there being a heavy surf, she was soon almost bulged to pieces; but having thrown all the guns on one side overboard, and the tide flowing at the same time, she beat over the reef into a basin, and brought up in fourteen or fifteen fathoms; but she was so much damaged while on the reef, that, imagining she would go to pieces every moment, we had contrived to wrench ourselves out of our irons, and applied to the captain to have mercy on us, and suffer us to take our chance for the preservation of our lives; but it was all in vain—he was even so inhuman as to order us all to be put in irons again, though the ship was expected to go down every moment, being scarcely able to keep her under with all the pumps at work.

"In this miserable situation, with an expected death before our eyes, without the least hope of relief, and in the most trying state of suspense, we spent the night, the ship being by the hand of Providence kept up till the morning. The boats by this time had all been prepared: and as the captain and officers were coming upon the poop or roof of our prison, to abandon the ship, the water being then up to the combings of the hatchways, we again implored his mercy; upon which he sent the corporal and an armorer down to let some of us out of irons, but three only were suffered to go up, and the scuttle being then clapped on, and the master-at-arms upon it, the armorer had only time to let two persons out of irons, the rest, except three, letting themselves out; two of these three went down with them on their hands, and the third was picked up. She now began to keel over to port so very much, that the master-at-arms sliding overboard, and leaving the scuttle vacant, we all tried to get up, and I was the last out but three. The water was then pouring in at the bulk-head scuttles, yet I succeeded in getting out, and was scarcely in the sea when I could see nothing above it but the cross trees, and nothing around me but a scene of the greatest distress. I took a plank (being stark-naked) and swam towards an island about three miles off, but was picked up on my passage by one of the boats. When we got ashore to the small sandy key, we found there were thirty-five men drowned, four of whom were prisoners, and among these was my unfortunate messmate (Mr. Stewart); ten of us, and eighty-nine of the Pandora's crew, were saved.

"When a survey was made of what provisions had been saved, they were found to consist of two or three bags of bread, two or three beakers of water and a little wine; so we subsisted three days upon two wine glasses of water and two ounces of bread per day. On the 1st September we left the island, and on the 16th arrived at Coupang in the island of Timor, having been on short allowance eighteen days. We were put in confinement in the castle, where we remained till October, and on the 5th of that month were sent on board a Dutch ship bound for Batavia.

"Though I have been eight months in close confinement in a hot climate, I have kept my health in a most surprising manner, without the least indisposition, and am still perfectly well in every respect, in mind as well as in body; but without a friend, and only a shirt and pair of trousers to put on, and carry me home. Yet with all this I have a contented mind, entirely resigned to the will of Providence, which conduct alone enables me to soar above the reach of unhappiness."

This letter did not reach his mother until after the family had heard of his escape from the wreck of the Pandora, and were anxiously awaiting his arrival as a prisoner, and consequent trial on the charge of mutiny. His sister Nessy, an amiable and accomplished young lady, daily expecting her brother's arrival, addressed to him the following letter:—

"*Isle of Man*, 2d *June*, 1792.

"In a situation of mind only rendered supportable by the long and painful state of misery and suspense we have suffered on his account, how shall I address my dear, my fondly beloved brother!—how describe the anguish we have felt at the idea of his long and painful separation, rendered still more distressing by the terrible circumstances attending it! Oh! my ever dearest boy, when I look back to that dreadful moment which brought us the fatal intelligence that you had remained in the Bounty after Mr. Bligh had quitted her, and were looked upon by him as a *mutineer!*—when I contrast that day of horror with my present hopes of again beholding you, such as my most sanguine wishes could expect, I know not which is the most predominant sensation,—pity, compassion, and terror for your sufferings, or joy and satisfaction at the prospect of their being near a termination, and of once more embracing the dearest object of our affections.

"I will not ask you, my beloved brother, whether you are

innocent of the dreadful crime of mutiny: if the transactions of that day were as Mr. Bligh has represented them, such is my conviction of your worth and honor that I will, without hesitation, stake my life on your innocence. If, on the contrary, you were concerned in such a conspiracy against your commander, I shall be as firmly persuaded *his* conduct was the occasion of it; but, alas! could any occasion justify so atrocious an attempt to destroy a number of our fellow creatures? No, my ever dearest brother, nothing but conviction from your own mouth can possibly persuade me that you would commit an action in the smallest degree inconsistent with honor and duty; and the circumstance of your having swam off to the Pandora on her arrival at Tahiti (which filled us with joy to which no words can do justice), is sufficient to convince all who know you, that you certainly staid behind either by force or from views of preservation.

"How strange does it seem to me that I am now engaged in the delightful task of writing to you. Alas! my beloved brother, two years ago I never expected again to enjoy such a felicity, and even yet I am in the most painful uncertainty whether you are alive. Gracious God, grant that we may be at length blessed by your return! but, alas! the Pandora's people have been long expected, and are not even yet arrived. Should any accident have happened, after all the miseries you have already suffered, the poor gleam of hope with which we have been lately indulged will render our situation ten thousand times more insupportable than if time had inured us to your loss. I send this to the care of Mr. Hayward, of Hackney, father to the young gentleman you so often mention in your letters while you were on board the Bounty, and who went out as third lieutenant of the Pandora—a circumstance which gave us infinite satisfaction, as you would, on entering the Pandora, meet your old friend. On discovering old Mr. Hayward's residence, I wrote to him, as I hoped he would give me some information respecting the time of your arrival, and in return he sent me a most friendly letter, and promised this shall be given to you when you reach England, as I well know how great must be your anxiety to hear of us, and how much satisfaction it will give you to have a letter immediately on your return. Let me conjure you, my dearest Peter, to write to us the very first moment—do not lose a post—'t is of no consequence how short your letter may be, if it only informs us you are well. I need not tell you that you are the first and dearest object of our affections. Think, then, my adored boy, of the anxiety we must feel on your account; for my own part, I can know no real joy or happiness independent of you, and if any misfortune should now deprive us of you, my hopes of felicity are fled for ever.

"We are at present making all possible interest with every friend and connexion we have, to ensure you a sufficient support and protection at your approaching trial; for a trial you must unavoidably undergo, in order to convince the world of that innocence which those who know you will not for a moment doubt; but, alas, while circumstances are against you, the generality of mankind will judge severely. Bligh's representations to the Admiralty are, I am told, very unfavorable; and hitherto the tide of public opinion has been greatly in his favor. My mamma is at present well, considering the distress she has suffered since you left us; for, my dearest brother, we have experienced a complicated scene of misery from a variety of causes, which, however, when compared with the sorrow we felt on your account, was trifling and insignificant; *that* misfortune made all others light, and to see you once more returned and safely restored to us will be the summit of all earthly happiness.

"Farewell, my most beloved brother! God grant this may soon be put into your hands! Perhaps at this moment you are arrived in England, and I may soon have the dear delight of again beholding you. My mamma, brothers, and sisters, join with me in every sentiment of love and tenderness. Write to us immediately, my ever-loved Peter, and may the Almighty preserve you until you bless with your presence your fondly affectionate family, and particularly your unalterably faithful friend and sister,

(Signed) "NESSY HEYWOOD."

About the same time, this affectionate sister addressed a letter to her uncle, Commodore Pasley, and received the following reply:—

"*Sheerness, June* 8*th*, 1792.

"Would to God, my dearest Nessy, that I could rejoice with you on the early prospect of your brother's arrival in England. One division of the Pandora's people has arrived, and is now on board the Vengeance (my ship). Captain Edwards, with the remainder, and all the prisoners late of the Bounty, in number ten (four having been drowned on the loss of that ship), are daily expected. They have been most rigorously and closely confined since taken, and will continue so, no doubt, till Bligh's arrival. You have no chance of seeing him, for no bail can be offered.

"I cannot conceal it from you, my dearest Nessy, neither is it proper I should,—your brother appears by all accounts to be the greatest culprit of all, Christian alone excepted. Every exertion, you may rest assured, I shall use to save his life; but on trial I have no hope of his not being condemned. Three of the ten who are expected are mentioned in Bligh's narrative as men detained against their inclination. Would to God your brother had been one of that number! I will not distress you more by enlarging on the subject; as intelligence arises on their arrival, you shall be made acquainted. Adieu, my dearest Nessy. Present my affectionate remembrances to your mother and sisters, and believe me always, with the warmest affection,

"Your uncle, THOS. PASLEY."

How different is this from the letter of Bligh! while it frankly apprizes this amiable lady of the real truth of the case, without disguise, as it was then understood to be from Mr. Bligh's representations, it assures her of his best exertions to save her brother's life. Every reader of sensibility will sympathize in the feeling displayed in her reply.

"*Isle of Man*, 22*d June*, 1792.

"Harassed by the most torturing suspense, and miserably wretched as I have been, my dearest uncle, since the receipt of your last, conceive, if it is possible, the heartfelt joy and satisfaction we experienced yesterday morning, when, on the arrival of the packet, the dear delightful letter from our beloved Peter (a copy of which I send you enclosed) was brought to us. [This refers to the letter addressed to his mother, from Batavia.] Surely, my excellent friend, you will agree with me in thinking there could not be a stronger proof of his innocence and worth, and that it must prejudice every person who reads it most powerfully in his favor. Such a letter, in less distressful circumstances than those in which he writes, would, I am persuaded, reflect honor on the pen of a person much older than my poor brother. But when we consider his extreme youth (only sixteen at the time of the mutiny, and now but nineteen), his fortitude, patience, and manly resignation under the pressure of sufferings and misfortunes almost unheard of, and scarcely to be supported at any age, without the assistance of that which seems to be my dear brother's greatest comfort, a quiet conscience and a thorough conviction of his own innocence,—when I add, at the same time, with real pleasure and satisfaction, that his relation corresponds in many particulars with the accounts we have hitherto heard of the fatal mutiny,—and when I also add, with inconceivable pride and delight, that my beloved Peter never was known to breathe a syllable inconsistent with truth and honor;—when these circumstances, my dear uncle, are all united, what man on earth can doubt of the innocence which could dictate such a letter? In short, let it speak for him. The perusal of his artless and pathetic story will, I am persuaded, be a stronger recommendation in his favor than anything I can urge.

"I need not tire your patience, my ever-loved uncle, by

dwelling longer on this subject (the dearest and most interesting on earth to my heart); let me conjure you only, my kind friend, to read it, and consider the innocence and defenceless situation of its unfortunate author, which calls for, and, I am sure, deserves all the pity and assistance his friends can afford him, and which, I am sure also, the goodness and benevolence of your heart will prompt you to exert in his behalf. It is perfectly unnecessary for me to add, after the anxiety I feel, and cannot but express, that no benefit conferred upon myself will be acknowledged with half the gratitude I must ever feel for the smallest instance of kindness shown to my beloved Peter. Farewell, my dearest uncle. With the firmest reliance on your kind and generous promises, I am ever, with the truest gratitude and sincerity,

"Your most affectionate niece,

"NESSY HEYWOOD."

As soon as the arrival of Heywood was known, the poor mother addressed him thus :—

"*Isle of Man, June 29th*, 1792.

"Oh! my ever dearly-beloved and long-lost son, with what anxiety have I waited for this period! I have counted the days, hours, and even minutes since I first heard of the horrid and unfortunate mutiny which has so long deprived me of my dearest boy: but now the happy time is come when, though I cannot have the unspeakable pleasure of seeing and embracing you, yet I hope we may be allowed to correspond; surely there can be nothing improper in a liberty of this sort between an affectionate mother and her dutiful and beloved son, who, I am perfectly convinced, was never guilty of the crime he has been suspected of by those who did not know his worth and truth. I have not the least doubt but that the all-gracious God, who of his good providence has protected you so long, and brought you safe through so many dangers and difficulties, will still protect you, and at your trial make your innocence appear as clear as light. All your letters have come safe to me, and to my very dear good Nessy. Ah! Peter, with what real joy did we all receive them, and how happy are we that you are now safe in England! I will endeavor, my dearest lad, to make your present situation as comfortable as possible, for so affectionate and good a son deserves my utmost attention. Nessy has written to our faithful and kind friend, Mr. Heywood, of Plymouth, for his advice, whether it would be proper for her to come up to you; if he consents to her so doing, not a moment shall be lost, and how happy shall I be when she is with you! Such a sister as she is! Oh! Peter, she is a most valuable girl," &c.

On the same day this "most valuable girl" thus writes:—

"My dearest and most beloved brother,—Thanks to that Almighty Providence which has so miraculously preserved you, your fond, anxious, and, till now, miserable Nessy, is at last permitted to address the object of her tenderest affection in England! Oh! my admirable, my heroic boy, what have we felt on your account! yet how small, how infinitely trifling was the misery of our situation when compared with the horror of yours! Let me now, however, with confidence hope that the God of all mercies has not so long protected you in vain, but will at length crown your fortitude and pious resignation to his will with that peace and happiness you so richly merit. How blest did your delightful and yet dreadful letter from Batavia make us all! Surely, my beloved boy, you could not for a moment imagine we ever supposed you guilty of the crime of mutiny. No, no; believe me, no earthly power could have persuaded us that it was possible for you to do any thing inconsistent with strict honor and duty. So well did we know your amiable, steady principles, that we were assured your reasons for staying behind would turn out such as you represent them; and I firmly trust that Providence will at length restore you to those dear and affectionate friends, who can know no happiness until they are blessed with your loved society. Take care of your precious health, my angelic boy. I shall soon be with you; I have written to Mr. Heywood (your and our excellent friend and protector) for his permission to go to you immediately, which my uncle Heywood, without first obtaining it, would not allow, fearing lest any precipitate step might injure you at present; and I only wait the arrival of his next letter to fly into your arms. Oh! my best beloved Peter, how I anticipate the rapture of that moment!—for, alas! I have no joy, no happiness, but in your beloved society, and no hopes, no fears, no wishes, but for you."

Mr. Heywood's sisters all address their unfortunate brother in the same affectionate but less impassioned strain; and a little trait of good feeling is mentioned, on the part of an old female servant, that shows what a happy and attached family the Heywoods were, previous to the melancholy affair in which their boy became entangled. Mrs. Heywood says,—

"My good honest Birket is very well, and says your safe return has made her more happy than she has been for these two-and-forty years she has been in our family."

The poor prisoner thus replies, from his majesty' ship Hector, to his "beloved sisters all:"—

"This day I had the supreme happiness of your long expected letters, and I am not able to express the pleasure and joy they afforded me; at the sight of them my spirits, low and dejected, were at once exhilarated; my heart had long and greatly suffered from my impatience to hear from those most dear to me, and was tossed and tormented by the storms of fearful conjecture—but they are now subsided, and my bosom has at length attained that long-lost serenity and calmness it once enjoyed; for you may believe me when I say it never yet has suffered any disquiet from my own misfortunes, but from a truly anxious solicitude for, and desire to hear of, your welfare. God be thanked, you still entertain such an opinion of me as I will flatter myself I have deserved; but why do I say so? Can I make myself too worthy the affectionate praises of such amiable sisters? Oh! my Nessy, it grieves me to think I must be under the necessity, however heart-breaking to myself, of desiring you will relinquish your most affectionate design of coming to see me: it is too long and tedious a journey, and even on your arrival you would not be allowed the wished-for happiness, both to you and myself, of seeing, much less conversing with, your unfortunate brother: the rules of the service are so strict, that prisoners are not permitted to have any communication with female relations; thus even the sight of, and conversation with, so truly affectionate a sister, is for the present denied me! The happiness of such an interview let us defer till a time (which, please God, will arrive,) when it can be enjoyed with more freedom, and unobserved by the gazing eyes of an inquisitive world, which in my present place of confinement would of course not be the case.

"I am very happy to hear that poor old Birket is still alive; remember me to her, and tell her not to *heave aback*, until God grants me the pleasure of seeing her.

"And now, my dear Nessy, cease to anticipate the happiness of personal communication with your poor but resigned brother, until wished-for freedom removes the indignant shackles I now bear from the feet of your fond and most affectionate brother,

"P. H."

On the 15th July, Commodore Pasley addressed the following business-like letter to Miss Heywood:—

"I received your letter, my dearest Nessy, with the enclosure [her brother's narrative], but did not choose to answer it until I had made a thorough investigation; that is, seen personally all the principal evidences, which has ever since occupied my whole thoughts and time. I have also had some letters from himself; and notwithstandiug he must still continue in confinement, every attention and indulgence possible is granted him by Captain Montague of the Hector, who is my particular friend. I have no doubt of the truth of your brother's narrative; the master, boatswain, gunner, and carpenter, late of the Bounty, I have seen, and have the pleasure to assure you that they are all favorable, and corroborate what he says. That *fellow*, Captain Edwards, whose inhuman rigor of confinement I shall never forget, I have likewise seen; he cannot deny that Peter avowed himself late of the Bounty when he came voluntarily aboard; this is a favorable circumstance. I have been at the Admiralty, and read over all the depositions taken and sent home by Bligh and his officers from Batavia, likewise the court-martial on himself; in none of which appears anything against Peter. As soon as Lieutenant Hayward arrives with the remainder of the Pandora's crew, the court-martial is to take place. I shall certainly attend, and we must have an able counsellor to assist, for I will not deceive you, my dear Nessy, however favorable circumstances may appear, our martial law is severe; by the tenor of it, the man who stands neuter is equally guilty with him who lifts his arm against his captain in such cases. His extreme youth, and his delivering himself up, are the strong points of his defence. Adieu! my dearest Nessy; present my love to your mother and sisters, and rest assured of my utmost exertions to extricate your brother.

"Your affectionate uncle,

"T. Pasley."

This excellent man did not stop here: knowing that sea-officers have a great aversion from counsel, he writes to say—

"A friend of mine, Mr. Graham, who has been secretary to the different admirals on the Newfoundland station for these twelve years, and consequently has acted as judge-advocate at courts-martial all that time, has offered me to attend you; he has a thorough knowledge of the service, uncommon abilities, and is a very good lawyer. He has already had most of the evidences with him. Adieu! my young friend; keep up your spirits, and rest assured I shall be watchful for your good. My heart will be more at ease if I can get my friend Graham to go down, than if you were attended by the first counsel in England."

Mr. Graham accordingly attended, and was of the greatest service at the trial.

Miss Heywood having in one of her letters inquired of her brother how tall he was, and having received information on this point, expressed some surprise that he was not taller. He replies,—

"And so you are surprised I am not taller!—Ah, Nessy! let me ask you this—suppose the last two years of *your* growth had been retarded by close confinement,—nearly deprived of all kinds of necessary aliment—shut up from the all-cheering light of the sun for the space of five months, and never suffered to breathe the fresh air (an enjoyment which Providence denies to none of his creatures) during all that time—and without any kind of exercise to stretch and supple your limbs—beside many other inconveniences which I will not pain you by mentioning—how tall should you have been, my dear sister?—answer, four feet nothing. But enough of nonsense."

Nessy expressed a strong desire to see her brother, but she was told that the rules of the service would not allow it; also, that it would agitate him, when he ought to be cool and collected, to meet his approaching trial. This was quite enough; but as for herself, she says,—

"No danger, no fatigue, no difficulties would deter me—I have youth, and health, and excellent natural spirits—these and the strength of my affection would support me through it all; if I were not allowed to see you, yet being in the same place which contains you would be joy inexpressible! I will not, however, any longer desire it, but will learn to imitate your fortitude and patience."

Among the numerous friends that interested themselves in the fate of this unhappy youth was his uncle Colonel Holwell. About a fortnight before the trial he writes to him thus:—

"21*st August*, 1792.

"My very dear Peter,

"I have this day received yours of the 18th, and am happy to find by its contents, that notwithstanding your long and cruel confinement you still preserve your health, and write in good spirits. Preserve it, my dear boy, awful as the approaching period must be even to the most innocent, but from which all who know you have not a doubt of your rising as immaculate as a new-born infant. I have known you from your cradle, and have often marked with pleasure and surprise the many assiduous instances (far beyond your years) you have given of filial duty and paternal affection to the best of parents, and to brothers and sisters who doted on you. Your education has been the best: and from these considerations alone, without the very clear evidence of your own testimony, I would as soon believe the Archbishop of Canterbury would set fire to the city of London as suppose you could, directly or indirectly, join in such an absurd piece of business. Truly sorry am I that my state of health will not permit me to go down to Portsmouth, to give this testimony publicly before that respectable tribunal where your country's laws have justly ordained you must appear; but consider this as the *touchstone*, my dear boy, by which your worth must be known. Six years in the navy myself and twenty-eight years a soldier, I flatter myself my judgment will not prove erroneous. That Power, my dear Peter, of whose grace and mercy you seem to have so just a sense, will not now forsake you. Your dear aunt is as must be expected in such a trying situation, but more from your present sufferings than from any apprehension of what is to follow," &c.

With similar testimonies and most favorable auguries from Commodore Pasley, the Rev. Dr. Scott of the Isle of Man, and others, young Heywood went to the long and anxiously expected trial, which commenced on the 12th September, and continued to the 18th of that month.

The last letter from his beloved Nessy previous to the awful event thus concludes :—

"May that Almighty Providence whose tender care has hitherto preserved you be still your powerful protector! may he instil into the hearts of your judges every sentiment of justice, generosity, and compassion! may hope, innocence, and integrity be your firm support! and liberty, glory, and honor your just reward! may all good angels guard you from even the appearance of danger! and may you at lengh be restored to us, the delight, the pride of your adoring friends, and the sole happiness and felicity of that fond heart which animates the bosom of my dear Peter's most faithful and truly affectionate sister.

"N. H."

The family of young Heywood in the Isle of Man had been buoyed up from various quarters with the almost certainty of his full acquittal. From the 12th Septem-

7

ber, when the court-martial first sat, till the 24th of that month, they were prevented by the strong and contrary winds, which cut off all communication with England, from receiving any tidings whatever. But while Mrs. Heywood and her daughters were fondly flattering themselves with everything being most happily concluded, one evening, as they were indulging these pleasing hopes, a little boy, the son of one of their particular friends, ran into the room, and told them in the most abrupt manner that the trial was over and all the prisoners condemned, but that Peter Heywood was recommended to mercy; he added, that a man whose name he mentioned had told him this. The man was sent for, questioned, and replied he had seen it in a newspaper at Liverpool, from which place he was just arrived in a small fishing boat, but had forgotten to bring the paper with him. In this state of doubtful uncertainty this wretched family remained another whole week, harassed by the most cruel agony of mind, which no language can express.

The suspense into which the afflicted family in the Isle of Man had been thrown by the delay of the packet, was painfully relieved on its arrival in the night of the 29th September, by the following letter from Mr. Graham to the Rev. Dr. Scott, which the latter carried to Mrs. Heywood's family the following morning.

" *Portsmouth, Tuesday, 18th September.*

" Sir,

" Although a stranger, I make no apology in writing to you. I have attended and given my assistance at Mr. Heywood's trial, which was finished and the sentence passed about half an hour ago. Before I tell you what that sentence is, I must inform you that his life is safe, notwithstanding it is at present at the mercy of the king, to which he is in the strongest terms recommended by the court. That any unnecessary fears may not be productive of misery to the family, I must add, that the king's attorney-general (who with Judge Ashurst attended the trial) desired me to make myself perfectly easy, for that my friend was as safe as if he had not been condemned. I would have avoided making use of this dreadful word, but it must have come to your knowledge, and, perhaps, unaccompanied by many others of a pleasing kind. To prevent its being improperly communicated to Mrs. or the Misses Heywood, whose distresses first engaged me in the business, and could not fail to call forth my best exertions upon the occasion, I send you this by express. The mode of communication I must leave to your discretion; and shall only add, that although, from a combination of circumstances, ill-nature, and mistaken friendship, the sentence is in itself terrible; yet it is incumbent on me to assure you, that, from the same combination of circumstances, everybody who attended the trial is perfectly satisfied in his own mind that he was *hardly guilty in appearance, in intention he was perfectly innocent.* I shall of course write to Commodore Pasley, whose mind, from my letter to him of yesterday, must be dreadfully agitated, and take his advice about what is to be done when Mr. Heywood is released. I shall stay here till then, and my intention is afterward to take him to my house in town, where, I think, he had better stay till one of the family calls for him: for he will require a great deal of tender management after all his sufferings; and it would perhaps be a necessary preparation for seeing his mother, that one or both his sisters should be previously prepared to support her on so trying an occasion."

On the following day Mr. Graham again writes to Dr. Scott, and among other things observes—

"It will be a great satisfaction to his family to learn, that the declarations of some of the other prisoners, since the trial, put it past all doubt that the evidence upon which he was convicted must have been (to say nothing worse of it) an unfortunate belief, on the part of the witness, of circumstances which either never had existence, or were applicable to one of the other gentlemen who remained in the ship, and not to Mr. Heywood."

This is supposed to refer to the evidence given by Hallet; who afterwards frequently expressed his deep regret that he had testified what on subsequent reflection he believed to be incorrect, viz., that during the mutiny Bligh said to Heywood something (the witness did not know what) upon which Heywood laughed, turned round, and walked away; he regretted having testified this, because he had subsequently satisfied himself, that, in the general confusion of the scene, he confounded Heywood with some other person.

On the 20th of September, Heywood addressed to Dr. Scott the first letter he wrote after his conviction.

"Honored and dear Sir,

"On Wednesday the 12th instant the awful trial commenced.

and on *that* day, *when in court*, I had the pleasure of receiving your most kind and parental letter; in answer to which I now communicate to you the melancholy issue of it, which, as I desired my friend Mr. Graham to inform you of immediately, will be no dreadful news to you. The morning lowers, and all my hope of worldly joy is fled. On Tuesday morning, the 18th, the dreadful sentence of death was pronounced upon me, to which (being the just decree of that Divine Providence who first gave me breath) I bow my devoted head with that fortitude, cheerfulness, and resignation, which is the duty of every member of the church of our blessed Saviour and Redeemer Christ Jesus. To him alone I now look for succor, in full hope that perhaps a few days more will open to the view of my astonished and fearful soul his kingdom of eternal and incomprehensible bliss, prepared only for the righteous of heart.

"I have not been found guilty of the slightest act connected with that detestable crime of mutiny, but am doomed to die for not being active in my endeavors to suppress it. Could the witnesses who appeared on the court-martial be themselves tried, *they* would also suffer for the very same and only crime of which I have been found guilty. But I am to be the victim. Alas! my youthful inexperience, and not depravity of will, is the sole cause to which I can attribute my misfortunes. But, so far from repining at my fate, I receive it with a dreadful kind of joy, composure, and serenity of mind; well assured that it has pleased God to point me out as a subject through which some greatly useful (though at present unsearchable) intention of the divine attributes may be carried into execution for the future benefit of my country. Then why should I repine at being made a sacrifice for the good, perhaps, of thousands of my fellow-creatures; forbid it, Heaven! Why should I be sorry to leave a world in which I have met with nothing but misfortunes and all their concomitant evils? I shall, on the contrary, endeavor to divest myself of all wishes for the futile and sublunary enjoyments of it, and prepare my soul for its reception into the bosom of its Redeemer. For though the very strong recommendation I have had to his majesty's mercy by all the members of the court may meet with his approbation, yet that is but the balance of a straw, a mere uncertainty, upon which no hope can be built; the other is a certainty that must one day happen to every mortal, and, therefore, the salvation of my soul requires my most prompt and powerful exertions during the short time I may have to remain on earth.

"As this is too tender a subject for me to inform my unhappy and distressed mother and sisters of, I trust, dear sir, you will either show them this letter, or make known to them the truly dreadful intelligence in such a manner as (assisted by your wholesome and paternal advice) may enable them to bear it with Christian fortitude. The only worldly feelings I am now possessed of are for their happiness and welfare; but even these, in my present situation, I must endeavor, with God's assistance, to eradicate from my heart, how hard soever the task. I must strive against cherishing any temporal affections. But, my dear sir, endeavor to mitigate my distressed mother's sorrow. Give my everlasting duty to her, and unabated love to my disconsolate brothers and sisters, and all my other relations. Encourage them, by my example, to bear up with fortitude and resignation to the Divine will, under their load of misfortunes, almost too great for female nature to support, and teach them to be fully persuaded that all hopes of happiness on earth are vain. On my own account I still enjoy the most easy serenity of mind; and am, dear sir, for ever, your greatly indebted, and most dutiful, but ill-fated,

"PETER HEYWOOD."

His next letter is to his dearly beloved Nessy.

"Had I not a strong idea that, ere this mournful epistle from your ill-fated brother can reach the trembling hand of my ever dear and much-afflicted Nessy, she must have been informed of the final issue of my trial on Wednesday morning, by my honored friend Dr. Scott, I would not now add trouble to the afflicted by a confirmation of it. Though I have indeed fallen an early victim to the rigid rules of the service, and though the jaws of death are once more opened upon me, yet do I not now, nor ever will, bow to the tyranny of base-born fear. Conscious of having done my duty to God and man, I feel not one moment's anxiety on my own account, but cherish a full and sanguine hope that perhaps a few days more will free me from the load of misfortune which has ever been my portion in this transient period of existence; and that I shall find an everlasting asylum in those blessed regions of eternal bliss where the galling yoke of tyranny and oppression is felt no more.

"If earthly majesty, to whose mercy I have been recommended by the court, should refuse to put forth its lenient hand and rescue me from what is fancifully called an ignominious death, there is a heavenly King and Redeemer ready to receive the righteous penitent, on whose gracious mercy alone I, as we all should, depend, with that pious resignation which is the duty of every Christian; well convinced, that without his express permission not even a hair of our head can fall to the ground.

"Oh! my sister, my heart yearns when I picture to myself the affliction, indescribable affliction, which this melancholy intelligence must have caused in the mind of my much honored mother. But let it be your peculiar endeavor to watch over her grief and mitigate her pain. I hope, indeed, this little advice

7*

from me will be unnecessary; for I know the holy precepts of that inspired religion, which, thank Heaven! have been implanted in the bosoms of us all, will point out to you, and all my dear relatives, that fortitude and resignation which are required of us in the conflicts of human nature, and prevent you from arraigning the wisdom of that omniscient Providence of which we ought all to have the fullest sense.

"I have had all my dear Nessy's letters; the one of the 17th this morning: but alas! what do they now avail? Their contents only serve to prove the instability of all human hopes and expectations; but, my dear sister, I begin to feel the pangs which you must suffer from the perusal of this melancholy paper, and will therefore desist, for I know it is more than your nature can support. The contrast between last week's correspondence and this is great indeed; but why? we had only hope then; and have we not the same now? certainly. Endeavor, then, my love, to cherish that hope, and with faith rely upon the mercy of that God, who does as to him seems best and most conducive to the general good of his miserable creatures.

"Bear it then with Christian patience, and instil into the mind of my dear and now sorrowful sisters, by your advice, the same disposition; and, for Heaven's sake, let not despair touch the soul of my dear mother—for then all would be over. Let James also employ all his efforts to cheer her spirits under her weight of woe. I will write no more. Adieu, my dearest love! Write but little to me, and pray for your ever affectionate but ill-fated brother.

"P. S. I am in perfect spirits; therefore let not your sympathizing feelings for my sufferings hurt your own precious health, which is dearer to me than life itself. Adieu!"

From this time a daily correspondence passed between Peter Heywood and his sister Nessy, the latter indulging hope, even to a certainty, that she should not be deceived,—the other preaching up patience and resignation, with a full reliance on his innocence and integrity. "Cheer up, then," says he, "my dear Nessy; cherish *your hope*, and I will exercise *my patience*." Indeed, so perfectly calm was this young man under his dreadful calamity, that in a very few days after condemnation his brother says, "While I write this, Peter is sitting by me making a Tahitian vocabulary, and so happy and intent upon it, that I have scarcely an opportunity of saying a word to him; he is in excellent spirits, and I am convinced they are better and better every day."

This vocabulary is a very extraordinary performance; it consists of one hundred full-written folio pages; the words alphabetically arranged, and all the syllables accented. It appears from a passage in the "Voyage of the Duff," that a copy of this vocabulary was of great use to the missionaries who were first sent to Tahiti in this ship. By the aid of the vocabulary they during their voyage arranged a number of sentences according to the English idiom, which they supposed would be serviceable in intercourse with the Tahitians; soon after landing, however, they found it would be necessary to discontinue the use of them.

As soon as the sentence of the court was known, many friends of Heywood interested themselves to secure a happy issue of the recommendation to mercy; but for nearly another month the family were suffered to remain in the most painful state of suspense. At length, a day or two before the king's warrant was issued, Mr. Graham wrote the following to Peter's mother:—

"My dear Madam,

"If feeling for the distresses and rejoicing in the happiness of others denote a heart which entitles the owner of it to the confidence of the good and virtuous, I would fain be persuaded that mine has been so far interested in your misfortunes, and is now so pleased with the prospect of your being made happy, as cannot fail to procure me the friendship of your family, which, as it is my ambition, it cannot cease to be my desire to cultivate.

"Unused to the common rewards which are sought after in this world, I will profess to anticipate more real pleasure and satisfaction from the simple declaration of you and yours, that "we accept of your services, and we thank you for them," than it is in common minds to conceive; but, fearful lest a too grateful sense should be entertained of the friendly offices I have been engaged in (which, however, I ought to confess I was prompted to, in the first place, by a remembrance of the many obligations I owed to Commodore Pasley), I must beg you will recollect, that by sending to me your charming Nessy (and if strong affection may plead such a privilege, I may be allowed to call her *my* daughter also) you would have overpaid me if my trouble had been ten times and my uneasiness ten thousand times greater than they were, upon what I once thought the melancholy, but now deem the fortunate, occasion which has given me the happiness of her acquaintance. Thus far, my dear madam, I have written to please myself. Now, for what must please you; and in which, too, I have my share of satisfaction.

"The business, though not publicly known, is most certainly finished; and what I had my doubts about yesterday I am satisfied of to-day. Happy, happy, happy family! accept of my congratulations; not for what it is in the power of words to express, but for what I know you will feel, upon being told that your beloved Peter will soon be restored to your bosom with every virtue that can adorn a man, and ensure to him an affectionate, a tender, and truly welcome reception."

At the foot of this letter Nessy writes thus:—"Now, my dearest mamma, did you ever in all your life read so charming a letter? Be assured it is exactly characteristic of the benevolent writer. What would I give to be transported (though only for a moment) to your elbow, that I might see you read it? What will you feel, when you know assuredly that you may with certainty believe its contents? Well may Mr. Graham call us happy! for never felicity could equal ours! Don't expect connected sentences from me at present, for this joy makes me almost delirious. Adieu! love to all—I need not say be happy and blessed as I am at this dear hour, my beloved mother,

"Your most affectionate,

"N. H."

On the 24th of October the warrant was issued, granting a full pardon. Mr. Graham's impatience to complete the happiness of the family prompted him to hasten immediately to Portsmouth, in order to bring the beloved sufferer up to his house, where Peter and Nessy met each other on the morning of the 29th of October. Her feelings are expressed in the following:—

"*Great Russell-street, Monday morning, 29th October, half past ten o'clock—the brightest moment of my existence!*

"My dearest mamma,—I have seen him, clasped him to my bosom, and my felicity is beyond expression! In person he is almost even now as I could wish; in mind you know him an angel. I can write no more, but to tell you, that the three happiest beings at this moment on earth are your most dutiful and affectionate children,

"NESSY HEYWOOD.
"PETER HEYWOOD.
"JAMES HEYWOOD.

"Love to and from all ten thousand times."

This amiable young lady did not long survive her brother's liberty. This impassioned and most affectionate of sisters, with an excess of sensibility which acted too powerfully on her bodily frame, sunk, as is often the case with such susceptible minds, on the first attack of consumption. She died within the year of her brother's liberation.

But to return to Mr. Heywood. When the king's full and free pardon had been read to this young officer by Captain Montagu, with a suitable admonition and congratulation, he addressed that officer in the following terms,—so suitably characteristic of his noble and manly conduct throughout the whole of the distressing business in which he was innocently involved :—

> "Sir,—When the sentence of the law was passed upon me, I received it, I trust, as became a man; and if it had been carried into execution, I should have met my fate, I hope, in a manner becoming a Christian. Your admonition cannot fail to make a lasting impression on my mind. I receive with gratitude my sovereign's mercy, for which my future life shall be faithfully devoted to his service."

And well did his future conduct fulfil that promise. Notwithstanding the inauspicious manner in which the first five years of his servitude in the navy had been passed, two of which were spent among mutineers and savages, and eighteen months as a close prisoner in irons, in which condition he was shipwrecked and within an ace of perishing,—notwithstanding this unpromising commencement, he re-entered the naval service under the auspices of his uncle, Commodore Pasley, and Lord Hood, who presided at his trial, and who earnestly recommended him to embark again as a midshipman without delay, offering to take him into the Victory, under his own immediate patronage. In the course of this service, to qualify for the commission of lieutenant, he was under the respective commands of three or four distinguished officers who had sat on his trial, from all of whom he received the most flattering proofs of esteem and approbation.

He was subsequently intrusted with several commands,

F

and, during the long and arduous contest between England and France, he pursued an honorable career. In a note of his own writing it is stated, that on paying off the Montagu, in July, 1816, he came on shore, after having been actively employed *at sea* twenty-seven years, six months, one week, and five days, out of a servitude in the navy of twenty-nine years, seven months, and one day. Having reached nearly the top of the list of captains, he died in the year 1831, leaving behind him a high and unblemished character in that service of which he was a most honorable, intelligent, and distinguished member.

CHAPTER VII.

THE MUTINEERS' RETREAT.

* * * "Within him hell
He brings, and round about him, nor from hell
One step no more than from himself can fly
By change of place." * * *

"The chief and all his crew of life bereft,
Save one repentant still in mercy left,
Long since by painful forms of death had found,
That guilt, howe'er adroit, beyond the bound
Of God's permitting will cannot prevail,
Nor long, at best, to meet due vengeance fail."

But what has this long tale of five chapters about the bread-tree and the mutiny on board the ship Bounty, and the dreadful shipwreck of the Pandora, and the sufferings of the Heywoods, to do with the history of the little nation which was discovered in 1808, by Captain Folger, on Pitcairn's Island? In chapter first I promised that I would explain their origin and relate their history. And does not the reader already apprehend, that they descended from the party of mutineers that sailed away from Tahiti under Christian? When Christian and his party finally left Tahiti in the Bounty, they took with them each a wife, and also three other Tahitian women, with six islanders as men-servants, two being natives of Toobouai, and four of Tahiti. Where they were going no one knew. It was said that Christian intended to find some uninhabited island, where there should be no harbor for ships, run the Bounty ashore, take everything out of her, then destroy her entirely, and live and die on the island. This led Captain Edwards, in the Pandora, to visit so many islands; but his search, as has been mentioned in chapter fourth, was wholly in vain; and nothing more was ever heard respecting Christian and the other eight mutineers with him, although many inquiries had been made, and almost twenty years had elapsed, until Captain Folger visited Pitcairn's Island, and went ashore to see Aleck, and had with him that interesting conversation which was noticed in chapter first.

Aleck stated that his true name was Alexander Smith, and that he was one of the crew of the Bounty. He related to Captain Folger the whole of their proceedings from the time of the mutiny. He stated that the leader of the mutiny was Fletcher Christian, who had a quarrel with the commander, and the very first night after it, plotted the mutiny and induced some others to join him. Smith's account of the subsequent course of the mutineers, down to the time of the separation of the sixteen from Christian and the eight who left Tahiti in the Bounty on the 21st of September, 1789, agreed entirely with what has been related in chapter fifth.

When Christian and his comrades left Tahiti they bade farewell to the world; but they had not decided what unfrequented spot they would seek in which to spend their days. The Marquesas Islands were first mentioned; but Christian, on reading Captain Carteret's account of Pitcairn's Island, thought it better adapted to the purpose, and accordingly shaped a course thither. They reached it not many days afterwards; and Christian, with one of the seamen, landed in a little nook, the most convenient that could be found for disembarkation. They soon traversed the island sufficiently to be satisfied that it was exactly suited to their wishes. It possessed water, wood, a good soil, and some fruits. The anchorage in the offing was very bad, and landing for boats extremely hazardous. The mountains were so difficult of access, and the passes so narrow, that they might be maintained by a few persons against an army; and there were several caves, to which, in case of necessity, they could retreat, and where, as long as their provision lasted, they might bid defiance to their pursuers. With this intelligence they returned on board, and brought the ship to an anchor in a small bay on the northern side of the island, (the same that was afterwards named *Bounty Bay*,) where everything that could be of utility was landed, and where it was agreed to destroy the ship, either by running her on shore or burning her. Christian, Smith, and the majority, were for the former expedient; but while they went to the forepart of the ship, to execute this business, Matthew Quintal set fire to the carpenter's store-room. The vessel burnt to the water's edge, and then drifted upon the rocks, where the remainder of the wreck was burnt for fear of discovery. This occurred on the 23d of January, 1790.

Upon their first landing they perceived, by the remains of several habitations, morais, and three or four rudely sculptured images, which stood upon the eminence overlooking the bay where the ship was destroyed, that the island had been previously inhabited. Some apprehensions were, in consequence, entertained lest the natives should have secreted themselves, and might in some unguarded moment make an attack upon them; but by degrees these fears subsided, and their avocations proceeded without interruption.

A suitable spot of ground for a village was fixed upon, with the exception of which the island was divided into equal portions, but to the exclusion of the poor blacks, who being only friends of the seamen, were not considered as entitled to the same privileges. Obliged to lend their assistance to the others in order to procure a subsistence, they thus, from being their friends, in the course of time became their slaves. No discontent, however, was manifested, and they willingly assisted in the cultivation of the soil. In clearing the space that was allotted to the village, a row of trees was left between it and the sea, for the purpose of concealing the houses from the observation of any vessels that might be passing, and nothing was allowed to be erected that might in any way attract attention. Until these houses were finished, the sails of the Bounty were converted into tents; and when no longer required for that purpose, became very acceptable as clothing. Thus supplied with all the necessaries of life, and some of its luxuries, they felt their condition comfortable even beyond their most sanguine expectation, and everything went on peaceably and prosperously for about two years, at the expiration of which, Williams, who had the misfortune to lose his wife about a month after his arrival, by a fall from a precipice while collecting birds' eggs, became dissatisfied, and threatened to leave the island in one of the boats of the Bounty, unless he had another wife; an unreasonable request, as it could not be complied with, except at the expense of the happiness of one of his companions: but Williams, actuated by selfish considerations alone, persisted in his threat, and the Europeans not willing to part with him, on account of his usefulness as an armorer, constrained one of the blacks to bestow his wife upon the applicant. The blacks, outrageous at this second act of flagrant injustice, made common cause with their companion, and matured a plan of revenge upon their aggressors, which, had it succeeded, would have proved fatal to all the Europeans. Fortunately, the secret was imparted to the women, who ingeniously communicated it to the white men in a song, of which the words were, "Why does black man sharpen axe? to kill white man." The plot being thus discovered, the husband who had his wife taken from him, and another whom Christian had shot at, (though, it is stated, with powder only,) fled into the woods, and were treacherously murdered by their countrymen on the promise of pardon for the perpetration of this foul deed.

Tranquillity being thus restored, matters went on tolerably well for a year or two longer; but the oppression and ill treatment which the Tahitians received, more particularly from Quintal and M'Koy, the most active and determined of the mutineers, drove them to the for-

8

mation of another plot for the destruction of their oppressors, which was too successfully executed. A day was fixed for attacking and putting to death all the Englishmen while at work in their respective plantations. Williams was the first man that was shot. They next proceeded to Christian, who was working at his yam-plot, and shot him. Mills, confiding in the fidelity of his Tahitian friend, stood his ground, and was murdered by him and another. Martin and Brown were separately attacked and slain, one with a maul, the other with a musket. Smith was wounded in the shoulder, but succeeded in making terms with the Tahitians, and was conducted by them to Christian's house, where he was kindly treated. Young, who was a great favorite of the women, was secreted by them during the attack, and afterward carried to Christian's house. M'Koy and Quintal, who had been the most abusive, escaped to the mountains. Here this day of bloodshed ended, leaving only four Englishmen alive out of nine. It was a day of emancipation to the blacks, who were now masters of the island, and of humiliation and retribution to the whites.

There were now surviving four male Tahitians and four Englishmen; two of the latter, however, concealing themselves in the mountains. At the expiration of a week, the men of color now began to quarrel about choosing the women whose European husbands had been murdered; the result of which was the destruction of the whole of the former, some falling by the hands of the women, and one of them by Young, who, it would seem, coolly and deliberately shot him. Smith now proceeded into the mountains, to communicate the fatal intelligence to the two Europeans, M'Koy and Quintal, who, after some solicitation, returned to the village. Thus, in October, 1793, there were left upon the island the four Englishmen, with ten Tahitian women and some children. It is no wonder the most of these women were discontented, and were desirous to leave the island. They had been decoyed on board the Bounty by Christian, and since their residence on Pitcairn's Island had found little to make them happy. In 1794, so strongly did they urge their wishes to depart, that the men built them a boat, but on being launched, it immediately upset, and was found useless. The women continued dissatisfied, and being often abused by M'Koy and Quintal, they at length formed a new conspiracy, purposing to kill all the men in their sleep. This, however, was defeated by a seasonable discovery of the plot. Shortly afterwards the women actually made an assault on the men, but it terminated without any lives being lost, and they were all pardoned on the promise of future good behavior.

M'Koy had formerly been employed in a distillery in Scotland, and being much addicted to ardent spirits, he made experiments for the purpose of obtaining it from the root of a plant found upon the island called the *Ti*, or *Tee*, (*dracæna terminalis*,) and on the 20th of April, 1798, succeeded in producing a bottle of intoxicating liquor. This success induced his companion Quintal to turn his kettle into a still. The consequence was, that these two men were in a constant state of drunkenness, particularly M'Koy; on whom, it seems, it had the effect of producing fits of delirium; and in one of these he threw himself from a cliff and was killed on the spot. The melancholy fate of this man created so forcible an impression on the remaining few, that they resolved never again to touch spirits.

Some time in the following year, that is, about 1799, Quintal lost his wife by a fall from the cliff, while in search of birds' eggs; he grew discontented, and, though there were several disposable women on the island, and he had already experienced the fatal effects of a similar demand, nothing would satisfy him but the wife of one of his companions. Of course neither of them felt inclined to accede to this unreasonable demand; and he sought an opportunity of putting them both to death. He was fortunately foiled in his first attempt, but swore openly he would speedily repeat it. Smith and Young, having no doubt he would follow up his intention, and fearing he might be more successful in the next attempt, came to the resolution that, as their own lives were not safe while he was in existence, they were justified in putting him to death, which they did by felling him with a hatchet.

Smith and Young were now the sole survivors out of the fifteen males that had landed upon the island. Young was a man of some education, and of a serious turn of mind; and it would have been wonderful, after the many dreadful scenes at which they assisted, if the solitude and tranquillity that ensued had not awakened feelings of remorse or disposed them to repentance. They had a Bible and a Prayer Book, which were found in the Bounty, and they read the church service regularly every Sunday. They now resolved to have morning and evening family prayers, and to instruct the children, who at that time amounted to nineteen. Young, however, was not long suffered to survive his repentance. An asthmatic complaint terminated his existence about a year after the death of Quintal; and Smith was now left the sole survivor of the guilty and misguided mutineers of the Bounty. The loss of his last companion was a great affliction to him, and was for some time most severely felt. It was a catastrophe, however, that more than ever disposed him to repentance, and determined him to execute the resolution he had made, in the hope of expiating his offences. His reformation could not, perhaps, have taken place at a more propitious moment. Out of nineteen children upon the island, there were several between the ages of seven and nine years; who, had they been longer suffered to follow their own inclinations, might have acquired habits which it would have been difficult, if not impossible, to eradicate. The moment was therefore most favorable for his design, and his laudable exertions were attended by advantages both to the objects of his care and to his own mind, which surpassed his most sanguine expectations. He, nevertheless, had an arduous task to perform. Besides the children to be educated, the Tahitian women were to be converted; and as the example of the parents had a powerful influence over their children, he resolved to make them his first care. Here also his labors succeeded; the Tahitians were naturally of a tractable disposition, and gave him less trouble than he anticipated; the children also acquired such a thirst after scriptural knowledge, that in a short time he had little else to do than to answer their inquiries and put them in the right way.

These efforts of Smith, or Aleck, as the young men called him, may lead us to believe that he had truly repented of his former bad conduct, and of all his sins in the sight of God. I do not know that he really had, because repentance is spiritual change in the heart as well as an outward reformation, and God only knows the heart; yet so great an alteration in his whole manner of life seems to furnish evidence of sincere penitence; and every one will rejoice to believe that Aleck became a pious Christian and obtained forgiveness of God through the blood of Jesus Christ. He had continued his faithful care of his increasing family to the time of Captain Folger's arrival, when the whole population, being about thirty-five in number, acknowledged him as their Father and Governor. The three young men that came out to Captain Folger in the boat (as mentioned in chapter first) were children of the mutineers, and there were others then grown up young men and women.

Smith had been on the island eighteen years, during all which time no ship had visited it. The first that was seen by him appeared off the island on the 27th of December, 1795; she did not approach near enough to enable him to make out to what nation she belonged; but he and his surviving comrades (four of the mutineers were then living) were greatly alarmed, probably fearing that they might be seized and carried to England and punished for their crimes. A second and a third ship had subsequently appeared, but neither of them attempted to communicate with the island; although the latter came so near as to show that the people on board had descried the inhabitants, and Aleck, through fear that he might be seized, fled and concealed himself in a cavern situated under a hill. The fourth was the Topaz, the vessel commanded by Captain Folger. It was not strange that Aleck was still under the influence of some fear that he might be seized and carried to England as a prisoner, and was therefore (as mentioned in chapter

8*

first) unwilling to go on board. Nor it is strange that, after that fear subsided, he was desirous to hear from the captain what was going on in the world. Being asked if he had heard of the great battles between the English and French fleets, he answered, "How could I, unless the birds of the air had been the heralds?" Captain Folger gave him an account of the victory of Nelson off Cape Trafalgar in 1805, and some other important victories, gained by the English. Aleck listened with attention, and at length becoming greatly elated at the success of his countrymen, raised his hat, and cried out, "Old England forever!" to the surprise and amusement of the young islanders, who probably had never seen their patriarch so much excited.

The people were very reluctant to part with their visitor. When Captain Folger was about to leave the island, they gathered around him with the warmest affection. Aleck gave him two instruments which had belonged to the ship Bounty, a compass used in steering the ship, and a golden time-piece called a chronometer. The young women brought presents of cloth made with their own hands and dyed with beautiful colors. He wished to decline taking all that was offered in the overflow of friendship, but Smith told him it would hurt their feelings, and the gifts could well be spared from the island. He made to them as suitable a return of presents as his ship afforded, and left them amidst their earnest prayers for his welfare. Their simple and amiable manners made a deep impression on his feelings, and, as he remarked afterwards to a friend, reminded him of Paradise more than any picture ever drawn by the imagination.

Some years afterwards Captain Folger sent to the Lords of the Admiralty, who manage the affairs of the English navy, the compass received from Aleck, and also a letter, a part of which is here inserted.

"*March 1st*, 1813."

"My Lords,

"The remarkable circumstance, which took place on my last voyage to the Pacific ocean, will, I trust, plead my apology for addressing your Lordships at this time. In February, 1808, I touched at Pitcairn's Island. My principal object was to procure seal skins for the China market; and from the account given of the island in Captain Carteret's voyage, I supposed it was uninhabited; but on approaching the shore in my boat, I was met by three young men in a double canoe, with a present, consisting of some fruit and a hog. They spoke to me in the English language, and informed me that they were born on the island, and their father was an Englishman who had sailed with Captain Bligh. After discoursing with them a short time, I landed with them, and found an Englishman, of the name of Alexander Smith, who informed me he was one of the Bounty's crew, and after putting Captain Bligh in the boat, with half the ship's company, they returned to Tahiti, where part of the crew chose to tarry; but Christian, with eight others, including himself, preferred going to a more remote place, and after making a short stay at Tahiti, where they took wives, and six men servants, proceeded to Pitcairn's Island, where they destroyed the ship, after taking everything out of her, which they thought would be useful to them. I remained but a short time on the island, and on leaving it Smith presented me with a time-piece and an azimuth compass, which he told me belonged to the Bounty. The time-keeper was taken from me by the governor of the island of Juan Fernandez, after I had it in my possession about six weeks. The compass I put in repair on board my ship, and I made use of it on my homeward passage, since which a new card has been put to it by an instrument maker in Boston. I now forward it to your Lordships, thinking there will be a kind of satisfaction in receiving it, merely from the extraordinary circumstances attending it.

"MAYHEW FOLGER."

The next information received concerning Aleck and his interesting family was obtained about six years after Captain Folger left them, by two English vessels which fell in with Pitcairn's Island in the year 1814; an account of their visit will be given in the next chapter.

CHAPTER VIII.

THE NEW NAME.

"What unexpected sounds are these
 That break upon the Briton's ears?
Rude children born in southern seas
 Speaking in his own tongue he hears.
A wondrous story, too, they tell;
 The Bounty's mutineers their sires;
On yonder isle, the offspring dwell
 Enjoying all their heart desires.
What more the Briton seeks to know,
He must of good *John Adams* learn."

The English vessels which visited Pitcairn's Island in 1814, were the Briton, commanded by Sir Thomas Staines, and the Tagus, commanded by Captain Pipon. The captains, having supposed the island to be uninhabited, were greatly surprized on approaching it to see regular gardens and neat houses, and especially to be addressed in their native language. When the ships were about two miles from the island, two young men were observed bringing their canoes on their shoulders down to the shore: they soon launched them, dashed through the heavy surf, and paddled off to the ships, and on their near approach, to the astonishment of those on board, cried out in English, "Wont you heave us a rope now?"

One of these young men was a son of Christian, and the first person that was born on the island; his name was Thursday October, so called, I suppose, from the day and month in which he was born. He was nearly twenty-five years old, very fine looking, about six feet high, with deep black hair, an open and frank countenence, and a complexion of a brownish cast. On page 93 is a representation of young Christian, drawn by Mr. Shillibeer, who was a lieutenant of marines on board the Briton. The hat worn by Christian was of straw, ornamented by black cock's feathers. His open coun-

Thursday October Christian.

tenance, well shaped muscular limbs, and fine figure, attracted general admiration. He said he was married to a woman much older than himself, one of those that accompanied his father from Tahiti. The other youth was called George Young; he was of handsome appearance and very interesting manners; a son of midshipman Young, one of the mutineers. Some others soon reached the ship in canoes. As soon as it was known in the ship that these unexpected visiters were descendants of the crew of the Bounty, a scene of thrilling interest took place on board the Briton; a circle was instantly gathered around them, and numerous questions were asked with eager curiosity. Lieutenant Shillibeer gives the following account of the questions and answers.

Question.—Christian, you say, was shot? *Answer.*—Yes, he was.

Q.—By whom? *A.*—A black fellow shot him.

Q.—What cause do you assign for the murder? *A.*—I know no reason, except a jealousy which I have heard then existed between the people of Tahiti and the English—Christian was shot in the back while at work in his yam plantation.

Q.—What became of the man who killed him? *A.*—Oh! that black fellow was shot afterwards by an Englishman.

Q.—Was there any other disturbance between the Tahitians and English, after the death of Christian? *A.*—Yes, the black fellows rose, shot two Englishmen, and wounded John Adams, who is now the only remaining man who came in the Bounty.

Q.—How did Adams escape being murdered? *A.*—He hid himself in the wood, and the same night, the women, enraged at the murder of the English, to whom they were more partial than their countrymen, rose and put every Tahitian to death in their sleep. This saved Adams; his wounds were soon healed, and although old, he now enjoys good health.

Q.—How many men and women did Christian bring with him in the Bounty? *A.*—Nine white men, six from Tahiti, and eleven or twelve women.

Q.—And how many are there now on the island? *A.*—In all we have forty-eight.

Q.—Have you ever heard Adams say how long it is since he came to the island? *A.*—I have heard it is about twenty-five years ago.

Q.—And what became of the Bounty? *A.*—After everything useful was taken out of her, she was run on shore, set fire to, and burnt.

Q.—Have you ever heard how many years it is since Christian was shot? *A.*—I understand it was about two years after his arrival at the island.

Q.—What became of Christian's wife? *A.*—She died soon after Christian's son was born, and I have heard that Christian took forcibly the wife of one of the black fellows to supply her place, and which was the chief cause of his being shot.

Q.—Then, Thursday October Christian is the oldest on the island, except John Adams, and the old women? *A.*—Yes, he is the first born on the island.

Q.—At what age do you marry? *A.*—Not before nineteen or twenty.

Q.—Are you allowed to have more than one wife? *A.*—No! we can have but one, and it is wicked to have more.

Q.—Have you been taught any religion? *A.*—Yes, a very good religion.

Q.—In what do you believe? *A.*—"I believe in God the Father Almighty, Maker of Heaven and earth: and in Jesus Christ his only Son our Lord; who was conceived by the Holy Ghost, Born of the Virgin Mary, Suffered under Pontius Pilate, Was crucified, dead, and buried; He descended into Hell; The third day he rose from the dead; He ascended into Heaven, And sitteth at the right hand of God the Father Almighty; From thence he shall come to judge the quick and the dead: I believe in the Holy Ghost; The holy Catholic Church; The communion of Saints; The forgiveness of sins; The resurrection of the body, and the life everlasting. Amen."

Q.—Who first taught you this belief? *A.*—John Adams says it was first by F. Christian's order, and that he likewise caused a prayer to be said every day at noon.

Q.—And what is the prayer? *A.*—It is,—"I will arise and go to my father, and say unto him, Father, I have sinned against Heaven, and before thee, and am no more worthy of being called thy son."

Q.—Do you continue to say this every day? *A.*—Yes, we never neglect it.

Q.—What language do you commonly speak? *A.*—Always English.

Q.—Do you understand the Tahitian? *A.*—Yes, but not so well.

Q.—Do the old women speak English? *A.*—Yes, but not so well as they understand it; their pronunciation is not good.

Q.—What countrymen do you call yourselves? *A.*—Half English, and half Tahiti.

Q.—Who is your king? *A.*—Why, King George, to be sure.

Q.—Have you ever seen a ship before? *A.*—Yes, we have seen four from the Island, but only one stopped. Mayhew Folger was the captain.

If the astonishment of the British officers was great on making this extraordinary (and, as they then thought, the first) discovery of a people who had been so long forgotten, and in hearing the offspring of these offenders speaking the English language correctly, their surprise and interest were still more highly excited by what occurred when the young men went into the cabin; for when Sir Thomas Staines had taken them below and offered them something to eat, they rose up, and one of them, placing his hands together in a posture of devotion, pronounced distinctly and with emphasis, in a pleasing tone of voice, the words, "For what we are going to receive the Lord make us truly thankful." Probably Sir Thomas was not accustomed to think of God, or to ask the divine blessing on receiving food; as many persons, both at sea and on land, not only neglect to acknowledge their dependence on God when they eat, but wholly refuse to pray to him or read his word, although they cannot move or breathe without his help. The lieutenant above mentioned, alluding to this incident, says, "I must here confess I blushed when I saw nature in its most simple state, offer that tribute of respect to the Omnipotent Creator, which from an education I did not perform, nor from society had been taught its necessity. Ere they began to eat, on their knees, and with hands uplifted, did they implore permission to partake in peace what was set before them, and when they had eaten heartily, resuming their former attitude, offered a fervent prayer of thanksgiving for the indulgence they had just experienced. Our omission of this ceremony did not escape their notice, for Christian asked me whether it was not customary with us also. Here nature was triumphant, for I should do myself an irreparable injustice did I not with candor acknowledge, I was both embarrassed and wholly at a loss for a sound reply, and evaded this poor fellow's question by drawing his attention to the cow, which was then looking down the hatchway."

Captain Pipon mentions that the young men on first seeing a cow which was on board the vessel were somewhat alarmed, and expressed a doubt whether the animal was a huge goat or a horned hog. A little black terrier also at first excited some fear in Young, who, getting behind one of the officers, said, "It is a dog; I have heard of such an animal; will it bite?" but soon after exclaimed to Christian, "What a pretty little thing it is!"

As the captains were desirous to learn correctly the fate of Fletcher Christian and his deluded accomplices, they determined to go on shore and see the old man, to whom these youths referred under the name of John Adams. This was none other than Aleck, who had taken a new name. I do not certainly know the reason of this; but some persons have supposed, that after Captain Folger informed him that the ship Pandora was sent out to find the mutineers and carry them to England, Aleck felt more afraid than before, and did not like to go by the name of Smith; and that he took that of John Adams in consequence of what Captain Folger told him about the celebrated John Adams who was so active a friend of the Americans in their revolutionary war, and who became President of the United States next after Washington. The captains found the landing to be difficult, and not wholly free from danger; but with the assistance of their able conductors, they passed the surf among the rocks and reached the shore without any other inconvenience than a complete wetting. They then ascended a rocky eminence, where they were received by a daughter of Adams. She had taken her post of observation there, probably, as a spy, in order to give her father notice if there should be any indication that the captains were intending to seize him; so that he might escape by fleeing, as on a former occasion, to the cavern under the hill. They were soon conducted to the house of Adams. Both he and his wife, a very old woman, and nearly blind, were at first considerably alarmed; but Sir Thomas Staines, to set his mind at rest, assured him that, so far from having come to the island with any intention to seize him, they had not previously been aware of his existence. This relieved his apprehensions and those of all the people under him, who now manifested great joy at seeing the men who lived in the native country of their protector and father, when they no longer feared his being taken away. They hastened to entertain their visiters with yams, cocoanuts, and other fruits, and fine fresh eggs; and Adams proposed to kill and dress a hog, but the time would not allow the captains to remain for the intended feast. They, however, remained long enough to hear from his lips the same story, in substance, which has been given in the preceding chapter, and to become delighted with the condition of the people. During the six years which had elapsed since the visit of Captain Folger, they had continued as happy as when he was there; not an instance of immoral conduct had occurred, nor a single case of strife.

The impression on the minds of the English officers was so manifestly favorable, that old Aleck's fears of a seizure and trial seem to have given way to a rising desire to revisit his native land; and he even expressed a desire to be conveyed thither in one of the ships, and signified this to his little commonwealth assembled at his door. "Appalled at a request not less sudden than opposed to all their feelings," says one of the captains, "they were at a loss for a reply. His charming daughter, although inundated with tears, first broke the silence.

"'Oh do not, Sir,' said she, 'take from me my father! do not take away my best, my dearest friend.' Her voice failed her—she was unable to proceed—leaned her head upon her hand, and gave full vent to her grief. His wife, too, (a Tahitian) expressed a lively sorrow. The wishes of Adams soon became known among the others, who joined in pathetic solicitation for his stay on the island. Not an eye was dry—the big tear stood in those of the men—the women shed them in full abundance. I never witnessed a scene so fully affecting, or more replete with interest. To have taken him from a circle of such friends, would have ill become a feeling heart; to have forced him away in opposition to their joint and earnest entreaties, would have been an outrage on humanity.

"With assurances that it was neither our wish nor intention to take him from them against his inclination, their fears were at length dissipated. His daughter, too, had gained her usual serenity, but she was lovely in her tears, for each seemed to add an additional charm. Forgetting the unhappy deed which placed Adams in that spot, and seeing him only in the character he now is, at the head of a little community, adored by all, instructing all, in religion, industry and friendship, his situation might be truly envied, and one is almost inclined to hope that his unremitting attention to the government and morals of this extraordinary little colony, will ultimately prove an equivalent for the part he formerly took,—entitle him to praise—and, should he ever return to England, ensure him the clemency of that Sovereign he has so much injured."

Every one must be glad that the captains did not take Adams away, because it would have been so great a loss and injury to the little society, that was happy and virtuous under his guidance. It would have been no injustice to him if they had carried him to England to be tried according to the laws, because he had actually been guilty of joining in a mutiny. This sin had not been altered, at all, by the many years that had passed away since he committed it, nor by his repentance and good life afterwards; it was still the same guilty thing, and really deserved punishment. But it is proper, that men should extend mercy and pardon to their fellow men, when it will not encourage them, or others, to persevere in vice or crime; as God always is merciful, and forgives all sinners, whether old or young, who rightly believe in Christ.

The day on which the captains landed on the island was, by their reckoning, Saturday, the 17th of September; but by the reckoning of Adams, it was Sabbath, the 18th of September. Yet both reckonings were made correctly. Some of my young readers may ask, how is it possible that both should have been kept correctly? They will better understand this when they have studied astronomy, if they will consider properly the effects resulting from the motion of the earth upon its axis. But it may be sufficient to remark here, that this curious difference in the reckoning was because the ship Bounty went from England by the *eastern* route around the Cape of Good Hope, and the two captains went by the *western* around Cape Horn. Althoügh the captains came to the island twenty-four years later than the Bounty, that made none of the difference. For if two ships should now start from London at the same instant, and sail one by the *eastern* and the other by the *western* course, and reach Pitcairn's Island exactly together, their reckoning would differ by one day. The ship that took the eastern would count one day more than the one that took the western course. If they should pass by each other at the island and come back to London, each in the way by which the other went, they would differ *two* days in their reckoning. One of them would count one day less than the people of London, and the other one day more. For instance, if the people of London reckoned it to be Monday the 6th of August, one of the ships would reckon it Sunday, the 5th, and the other Tuesday, the 7th day. When Captain Beechey, on his voyage to Beering's Straits, arrived at Tahiti, it was, by his reckoning, Saturday, 18th of March, 1826; he had come from England around Cape Horn; but at the island the day was the Sabbath, March 19th; the reckoning being conformed to that of the missionaries who had first come to the island around the Cape of Good Hope.

When the English captains took their departure, they left with the islanders some tools, kettles, and such other articles as were most needed and as the high surf would permit them to land. One of the captains shortly after wrote to an officer of the British government giving some account of what they had witnessed. The following is a copy of the letter:—

" *Valparaiso*, 18*th October*, 1814.

" Sir,

" I have the honor to inform you, that on my passage from the Marquesas Islands to this port, on the morning of the 17th September, I fell in with an island where none is laid down in the Admiralty or other charts, according to the several chronometers of the Briton and Tagus. I therefore hove to, until daylight, and then closed to ascertain whether it was inhabited which I soon discovered it to be, and, to my great astonishment found that every individual on the island (forty in number) spoke very good English. They proved to be the descendants of the deluded crew of the Bounty, who, from Tahiti, proceeded to the above mentioned island, where the ship was burned.

"Christian appeared to have been the leader and sole cause of the mutiny in that ship. A venerable old man, named John Adams, is the only surviving Englishman of those who last quitted Tahiti in her, and whose exemplary conduct and fatherly care of the whole of the little colony could not but command admiration. The pious manner in which all those born on the island have been reared, the correct sense of religion which has been instilled into their young minds by this old man, has given him the preëminence over the whole of them, to whom they look up as the father of one and the whole family. A son of Christian was the first born on the island, now about twenty-five years of age, named Thursday October Christian; the elder Christian fell a sacrifice to the jealousy of a Tahitian man, within three or four years after their arrival on the island. The mutineers were accompanied thither by six Tahitian men and twelve women; the former were all swept away by desperate contentions between them and the Englishmen, and five of the latter died at different periods, leaving at present only one man (Adams) and seven women of the original settlers. The island must undoubtedly be that called Pitcairn, although erroneously laid down in the charts. We had the altitude of the meridian sun close to it, which gave us 25 deg. 4 min. S. latitude, and 130 deg. 25 min. W. longitude, by the chronometers of the Briton and Tagus. It produces in abundance, yams, plantains, hogs, goats, and fowls; but the coast affords no shelter for a ship or vessel of any description; neither could a ship water there without great difficulty. I cannot, however, refrain from offering my opinion, that it is well worthy the attention of our laudable religious societies, particularly that for propagating the Christian religion, the whole of the inhabitants speaking the Tahitian tongue as well as the English. During the whole of the time they have been on the island, only one ship has ever communicated with them, which took place about six years since, and this was the American ship Topaz, of Boston, Mayhew Folger, master. The island is completely iron-bound with rocky shores, and the landing in boats must be at all times difficult, although the island may be safely approached within a short distance by a ship.

"T. Staines."

This letter, whicn was received at the Admiralty in England, early in the year 1815, and that from Folger, which was received not long before, excited great interest respecting the island. It was reported that the

9*

English government designed to send out a ship to visit the little colony, to carry the king's pardon to Aleck, and to supply the people with such things as they might need to make them more comfortable and happy. Many Christians hoped the English would think especially to send them Bibles and other good books, and a teacher and minister. Whether the government really contemplated at that time any such mission is doubtful. But certain it is, that no one in England, on learning the story, ever wished to have Aleck brought to a trial for his part in the mutiny; although he had taken an active part, being one of the men who stood with arms over Lieutenant Bligh while Christian held the cord round that officer's hands and threatened him with death, if he did not keep silence. Most people felt as Aleck himself could not help thinking they would, when they contemplated his little colony on Pitcairn's Island. When one of his visiters asked him if he wished his existence to be kept a secret, he answered, "No," and, pointing to the band of youth around him, added, "Do you think any man could seek my life with such a picture as this before his eyes?"

That the reader may understand better what a picture it was that Aleck's visiters saw, I will attempt in the next chapter to describe the village in which the people lived, and their manners and customs at that time.

CHAPTER IX.

THE HAPPY VILLAGE.

* * * "The happy shores without a law;
* * * * *
Where all partake the earth without dispute,
And bread itself is gathered as a fruit;
Where none contest the fields, the woods, the streams;
The goldless age, where gold disturbs no dreams."

The village lies on the northern side of the island, on a plain, elevated more than two hundred feet above the ocean, on ground sloping to the sea, and commanding a distant view of the horizon. It forms an oblong square, adorned with a large grove of cocoanut trees, and an immense banyan, and presents a very pleasing appearance to an observer at sea. The houses, at the upper end of the square, farthest from the sea, are occupied by the Patriarch Aleck, or Adams, and his son-in-law. The house on the opposite side is the dwelling of Thursday October Christian, and is probably the same that was his father's. The interior of this square is a smooth, green lawn, which is fenced around so as to keep out the quadrupeds or four-footed animals, but the fowls are allowed to wander over it. To reach this interesting spot, you must land in a boat amidst the surf and foam of the ocean, which rolls in an everlasting swell on every side of the island; you must then ascend the rocks, which bind the shore and present an invincible barrier to an invading foe; next you will pass through delightful groves of bread-fruit, cocoa-nut, and doodoe trees, till finally you come to the open lawn, and the smiling village.

The houses were said by Captain Folger to be built like those of the natives of Tahiti and the Sandwich Isles; and the following is given as a description of a Sandwich Island house. Small trees, about as big as a man's arm, are cut of suitable length, and driven into the ground like stakes, or posts, to form the frame of the house on each of the *sides*. The height of the posts above the ground is about five or six feet. Along the tops of these side posts, a pole about an inch thick is placed, and to this pole every post is lashed with strings made of a kind of vine. For the roof, there are as many rafters as there are side posts, one resting on each post; they meet at the top of the house, and are fastened to a ridge pole with strings of vine. The ridge pole is supported at each end by a long post reaching from the ground to the peak of the roof. On each side of these two middle posts, are others for the *ends* of the house, like those for the sides, reaching from the ground to the outer rafters. Thus the frame of the house is made. The next thing is to cover it. Small round sticks are leashed to the posts and rafters, five or six inches apart, all over the frame, from the ground to the ridge pole. Then to these sticks a thatch of grass is tied with strings made from the husk of the cocoanut. The roof is also covered with large leaves, laid so as to help to throw off the rain. The floor is formed by merely putting on the ground mats, which are made by the women, of a species of rush or of palm, being braided by the hand. Such houses look extremely neat and pretty, but they are not very safe or durable. The winds and rains easily penetrate the roof and sides. There is great danger of setting them on fire, for if the blaze of a candle happens to touch the grass-thatch in dry weather, the whole house is instantly in a blaze. And if no accident at all happens, the house will last only four or five years.

The English captains who visited Pitcairn village, found, that the people had in their houses many articles of furniture, some of which were taken from the ship Bounty. There were beds, with neat coverings ; tables, and large chests to contain their clothes, and whatever they considered valuable.

They had also gardens and cultivated fields, which produced cocoanuts, bananas, bread fruit, yams, sweet potatoes, turnips, plantains, pumpkins and water-melons. The beauty and utility of the bread-fruit tree have been described on a preceding page (13) ; next to that the cocoanut tree is perhaps the most useful. The trunk is cylindrical, three or four feet in diameter at the root, and gradually tapering to the top ; and furnishes good timber and is suitable for various purposes. It grows erect, sometimes to the height of sixty or seventy feet, without a branch or leaf excepting at the top, and is crowned by a tuft of long green leaves and several bunches of fruit. The leaves are composed of strong stalks, twelve or fifteen feet long, with a number of long narrow-pointed leaflets, arranged alternately on each side. They are attached to the trunk by a strong, fibrous matting, extending half way round the trunk, and reaching two or three feet up the leaf, thus effectually protecting it against the violence of the winds. While the leaves are young this matting is of a beautiful and transparent white, and is by natives of the South Sea Islands often cut into long narrow strips and tied into bunches, with which they ornament their hair; by exposure to the air it becomes coarser, and assumes a yellowish color. The leaves may be plaited into bonnets, screens, and baskets, both neat and convenient. The fruit grows in bunches sometimes of twenty or thirty nuts, and there are sometimes six or seven bunches on a tree at the same time. The nut is covered with a tough fibrous bark, enclosing in a soft white shell a pint or a pint and a half of the fluid called cocoanut milk. No correct idea of the taste of this juice can be formed from what is found in the nuts brought to America, as they are old and the milk comparatively rancid. The shell is useful for making cups, and the fibres of the husk for making cordage. This tree will grow in any situation; on the barren sea-beach and the sun-burnt sides of the mountain, as in the most fertile valleys. The doodoe tree is also very useful; it is a large tree with a handsome blossom, and supplies ornaments for the ears and hair, and nuts containing oil, so that being strung upon sticks they serve the purpose of candles. The tee-plant is said to have been much cultivated; its leaves, which are broad and oblong, being the common food of the hogs and goats, and serving the natives for wrappers in their cooking; from the root a saccharine liquor, resembling molasses, may be obtained by baking it in the ground; from this root also may be made a tea, which, when flavored with ginger, (also found on the island,) is not unpleasant. A juice for flavoring the tea of the sick is made from the sugar-cane, (which, however, was not much cultivated,) by pounding the cane and boiling it with a little ginger and grated cocoanut. The yam is cultivated in the same manner as the potato is with us.

The implements or tools used by the people in agriculture were such as they had made themselves from the iron supplied by the Bounty; they were, the spade, the hoe, the crow-bar, and a sort of hatchet. They had no plow. The only animals on the island were hogs and goats, which were very numerous; the latter afforded abundance of milk. The young men that went on board the ship Briton knew no larger animal; and, as has been mentioned, were greatly surprised on seeing a cow, and were in doubt whether it was a great goat or a horned hog.

Besides manufacturing their implements for cultivating the ground, they were accustomed to make household furniture of a simple kind, also canoes and apparatus for catching fish, of which several kinds, of good flavor. are found on the coasts of the island.

They had no money ; but would barter or exchange one article for another for each other's help, and not to grow rich, or to get anything below its real value. Each family had its own property, and there was also a common stock, out of which any family might be assisted, if sick or unfortunate. Perfect honesty ruled in all their dealings ; and complete harmony and friendship pervaded the whole society. If a disagreement of opinion happened, which was seldom, it occasioned nothing further than a transient *quarrel of the mouth*, as they termed it, that was instantly settled and ended by a reference to Aleck. Their good disposition was illustrated by an incident related by Lieutenant Shillibeer, as having occurred while the young men were visiting the ship Briton. In their eagerness to get on board, several of their canoes had been suffered to go adrift. The canoes being brought back, the captain ordered that one of the islanders should remain in each. This occasioned the question on which of them that duty should devolve ; one of them, named M'Koy, remarked that he supposed they were all equally anxious to see the ship, and the fairest way would be to cast lots ; this was at once acceded to, and those to whom it fell to go into the boats departed without a murmur.

Although all were industrious, yet the young people were allowed to enjoy several amusements, such as jumping, hopping, running, and various similar feats of activity. Being thus active and industrious, they grew up with tall, athletic, and beautiful forms, with faces full of good humor and cheerfulness. The young women were objects of admiration, having fine English features, and teeth perfectly regular and white as ivory, and exhibiting a most honorable degree of modesty and bashfulness.

Both sexes labored in cultivating the ground; and when a young man had cleared up a sufficient quantity of land to support a family, he was allowed to marry. If a couple wished to be married, they obtained the consent of Adams, who united them by a marriage ceremony.

Their dress was very different from ours, being similar to that of the natives in most of the islands in the Pacific ocean. For the males, it was commonly a long piece of cloth wound about the middle of the body, leaving the shoulders, arms, and legs naked, and a sort of hat, ornamented sometimes with feathers. For the females, it usually consisted of two pieces of cloth; the one a kind of apron, but very short; the other a kind of shawl or mantle, much larger, thrown over the shoulders and hanging down to the ancles. The females sometimes used to wear a cap or turban prepared in a fashion at the same time simple and yet indicative of taste.

All the cloth is made by the elder females. It is not of linen, cotton, or wool, nor spun or woven. It is the bark of what is called the cloth tree, or paper mulberry tree. Of this there are groves cultivated expressly for its bark. The plant is kept trimmed to a single shoot or stem, and when it is two inches thick and ten or twelve feet high, it is cut down for use. The bark is taken from each plant in one piece. Some time after being taken from the wood, it is put in water, and left, until it is covered with a soft and sticky substance. It is then pounded, or beaten, on a plank, with square pieces of wood of the breadth of one's hand, hollowed out into grooves; and thus it forms a sort of cloth, which may be made of any thickness or any size by adding more bark. Its natural color is a sort of yellow, but they often dye it blue, red, or black, and cover it with pictures of beasts, birds, and fishes. This cloth is very perishable; it cannot be washed at all unless it has been soaked in oil; and those who wear it, must get a new suit of clothes every month.

The young people are taught to read and write. Aleck was the first instructor. Their books and paper were taken from the Bounty. The books formed a considerable library, and the paper was not all gone when the British captains were on the island. The girls and boys were asked both to read and write in presence of Captain Folger, that he might know what improvement they had made. There had been much difficulty in teaching them to read, because they had no suitable helps, excepting a few leaves of an old spelling-book; yet it is said that they read very well, particularly the girls.

But the thing for which they were under the greatest obligation to their leader and father, is, that he instructed them in religion. The Bible was among the books taken from the Bounty. They had also the English Episcopal Prayer-book, which they were taught how to use. At marriages, baptisms, and funerals, they had simple but becoming ceremonies. They were in the uniform habit of praying to Almighty God every morning, noon, and evening, and they never failed to implore his blessing and to return thanks whenever they ate. The Sabbath day was regularly kept in a most sacred manner; all work and amusement being stopped, and all the families being assembled together, for the sake of public worship and religious instruction. Old Aleck usually gave this instruction, to which the people listened attentively, hearing of the attributes of the invisible God, and learning to obey his laws and put their trust in his goodness through the crucified Redeemer. I do not by any means suppose that they were all real and pious Christians; but it must have been delightful to this man in his old age, after all his sufferings and dangers, and especially if he was truly penitent for his follies and sins, to witness in the family around him such a readiness to be taught, and to be guided in the ways of virtue and religion. How happy would it be for all families, if the parents and the children should always thus keep the Sabbath!

Such, briefly sketched, is the picture of Aleck's people, as described by Folger and the English captains. I do not know that the people on Pitcairn's Island spoke with another vessel, or saw another, until the summer of the year 1817, when an American ship visited them. I never heard the name of the ship. She gave the islanders a beautiful little boat, and carried away to another place a Tahitian woman, the widow of Isaac Martin, one of the mutineers. This woman, whose name was Jenny, gave an account of the island, that was afterwards published in a newspaper printed in New South Wales. The same ship took off the old kettle which Quintal had converted into a still. Aleck did well to send that article from the island. It is to be hoped that good people of every name will ere long agree to banish rum and all ardent spirits from their houses, and will resolve never to drink a drop of them unless given as a medicine in case of sickness. Many persons in our country made such a resolution several years ago, and have been heartily glad of it ever since.

The master of the next ship that stopped at the island had a most interesting visit. It was Captain Henderson, of the ship Hercules, in January, 1819. When he was about two miles from the shore, several of the young men rowed out to his vessel in the little American boat, early in the morning. On approaching near, the first thing they asked was, whether the vessel was a merchantman or a ship of war, American or English. On being answered that it was a trading ship under English colors from India, they desired to get on board.

The captain received them on board, being nine in number, and, after breakfast, went on shore with them. Aleck and his people met and welcomed him on the rocks of the beach. Captain Henderson then delivered to Aleck a box of books, which the London Missionary Society had sent, and a letter from Aleck's own brother living in London. Aleck's sight had failed him, so that he requested Captain Henderson to read to him his brother's letter. It contained an account of his relatives in England, and described the death of one of his sisters, which caused the old man to weep as he heard it.

Captain Henderson after this ascended the rocks, and was led through the groves of bread-fruit, cocoanut, plantain, and tee-trees to the village. He found the houses presenting an appearance uncommonly neat and clean, and observed that some had recently been erected

10

with two stories, of an appearance quite different from the description given by Captain Folger. Adams had three daughters living and one son, a lad about fourteen years old. There were also three children of Christian, Thursday October and two younger brothers. The whole number in the village was stated as being forty-five ; it was said, however, that there had been several births since the visit of Captain Staines, but not a single death. The people retained their habits of devotion, offering prayers morning, noon, and night, and always imploring a blessing and returning thanks at meals. They were enjoying a healthful climate and a fertile soil, but were in great want of implements of agriculture and utensils for cooking. When Captain Henderson departed, he left such presents as he had and they most needed. Among them were three sheep and a lamb of the South American breed, some wheat and potatoes for planting, a few spades, a number of plates, knives, and forks, and a few pairs of shoes. To Adams he gave a reading glass to help his eyes.

The Hercules sailed from the island to Calcutta, and the statements respecting the inhabitants made by Captain Henderson awakened at Calcutta so much interest for them, that three thousand rupees, or about fifteen hundred dollars, were given by charitable persons to procure for them implements of husbandry and other useful articles. The articles purchased with this money, besides the agricultural and mechanic tools, consisted of some live stock, two chests of fruit trees, one keg of marrow-fat peas, two boxes of various vegetables, and a quantity of seeds and stones for sowing and planting, suited to the soil and climate of the island.

These were sent by Captain Henderson himself, who expected to visit the island again as he returned from Calcutta to Chili. There were also sent, from the committee of a benevolent Society, a number of Tracts, Prayer-books, and Bibles, and with them the following letter :—

"*To John Adams and others of Pitcairn's Island.*

"Calcutta, July 15, 1819.'

"It is with peculiar pleasure that I take an opportunity of sending to you, by Captain Henderson, of the ship Hercules, a small stock of religious books, of which, probably, your society on Pitcairn's Island may stand much in need. They are a present from a committee of the Society for promoting Christian knowledge established in this country; and I am sure that the prayers of this committee attend their present, that the books may lead to the advancement of you all in religious knowledge, and in Christian holiness of life. You will find books of instruction fitted for all ages; and may God Almighty prosper you in the use of them.

"At some future time, perhaps not very distant, you may find opportunities of imparting the knowledge which you acquire to the natives of other islands, in which the name of Jesus Christ is not known; and may become blessed instruments in the hand of God for extending the knowledge of his Son our Lord. I trust that you will eagerly seize any such occasion; and that by the example of your own lives, and by bringing up your children in habits of piety and virtue, you will recommend the Christian Religion to others as the only means of attaining true happiness here and hereafter.

The committee would be very glad to hear of the welfare of your little Society; and I am, with every good wish and prayer, indeed,

"Yours, —— ——."

Not long after Captain Henderson's visits, other ships, both English and American, called at the island. A gentleman who was there in December, 1822, stated that the inhabitants were increased to fifty-four, and gave the following account of them :—

"John Adams, the patriarch of this interesting population, still lives, and continues to train them up in the principles of piety and virtue. Their condition presents a delightful picture of social happiness.

"The Bible is their directory, and most of those who are above ten years of age can read it. A considerable part of their time is employed in offering up praises to the Almighty. Nearly the whole of the Sabbath is spent in prayer, singing, and reading the holy Scriptures.

"Every morning at *four* o'clock they assemble in their respective habitations for family devotion. At *eleven* all the families meet together on the green in the front of their dwellings, when John Adams reads prayers and portions of the Scriptures, and one or two Psalms are sung. Before sunset, they assemble again. Afterwards they have family prayer, sing the *Evening Hymn*, and retire to rest."

Aleck now began to fear that it would be an injury to these worthy and innocent people, if a great many ships should visit them, because the sailors and other persons in them are often so wicked, and might set very bad examples before the youth. On this account he expressed to the gentleman just mentioned a great desire that a pious minister might be sent to take the charge of his dear family before he should die. The wishes of Aleck were made known to good people in England, but no minister was sent; and after waiting some time in vain, and having heard of the American missionaries on the Sandwich Islands, he applied to them for assistance.

The letter was written by a person who says that he had been persuaded by the people to remain on the island to aid in instructing them to read and write, and who, in his letter, expresses himself as if he had been afterwards awakened and brought to that repentance, which the gospel of Christ requires of all. How long he had been upon the island, or from what place he came, I do not know, excepting that it is said he was an Englishman left there by a whale fishing vessel. The following is the letter sent to the missionary, Mr. Bingham :—

" *Pitcairn's Island, July* 10, 1824.

" Reverend Sir,

" By the desire of John Adams, and the other inhabitants of this place, I write these few lines to inform you of our great need of a minister of the gospel; and should esteem it as a great kindness, if you would endeavor to help us with one as soon as possible, as we are now here as sheep without a shepherd.

" The inhabitants of this place are fast increasing, being at present fifty-nine. We use our poor and imperfect endeavors to worship our Maker; but still we are in great want of an ordained minister to administer the holy ordinance of baptism, and the Lord's Supper, and other services, and to instruct us in the performance of our duty.

" I stopped at this island by desire of the inhabitants to assist in instructing them to read and write. I thank the Lord, that since my arrival at this place I have been convinced of the errors of my past life; and my chief desire is to increase in the knowledge and love of God, and promote the good of others.

"When Captain Henderson arrived here in the ship Hercules, of Calcutta, and brought a supply of books and other articles, he brought a letter to say that a minister was shortly coming. It is now between five and six years since, and we hear of no one being sent; so if you would endeavor to send us one, you would greatly oblige us all. . And I think, by the help of God, it will be the means of saving many souls, and a blessing to the people. If we should have the happiness to see one arrive, we will make his residence as comfortable as is in our power.

"JOHN BUFFETT."

What answer Mr. Bingham made to this letter I have never heard, but it was not in his power to send to the colony a missionary. John Buffett, however, continued his labors as a teacher, and was there when Captain Beechey, commander of the English ship Blossom, visited the island in the year 1825. Another Englishman, also, John Evans, son of a coach-maker in London, had before that time settled among them, and was married to a daughter of John Adams.

In the next chapter the reader will have an account of Captain Beechey's visit.

CHAPTER X.

THE PATRIARCH'S LAST YEARS.

"No borrow'd joys; they are all our own,
While to the world we live unknown,
Or by the world forgot;
Monarchs! we envy not your state;
We look with pity on the great,
And bless our humble lot."

OF the above mentioned visit Captain Beechey has given, in his narrative of the voyage of the ship Blossom, a full account; the principal part of which is here presented to the reader.

"At one o'clock in the afternoon of the 4th of December, [1825,] we saw Pitcairn's Island, being south west by west half west, at a considerable distance. The interest which was excited by the announcement of Pitcairn's Island from the mast-head brought every person upon deck, and produced a train of reflections that momentarily increased our anxiety to communicate with its inhabitants; to see and partake of the pleasures of their little domestic circle; and to learn from them the particulars of every transaction connected with the fate of the Bounty: but in consequence of the approach of night, this gratification was deferred until the next morning, when, as we were steering for the side of the island on which Captain Carteret has marked soundings, in the hope of being able to anchor the ship, we had the pleasure to see a boat under sail hastening towards us. At first the complete equipment of this boat raised a doubt as to its being the property of the islanders, for we expected to see only a well-provided canoe in their possession, and we therefore concluded that the boat must belong to some whale-ship on the opposite side; but we were soon agreeably undeceived by the singular appearance of her crew, which consisted of old Adams and all the young men of the island.

"Before they ventured to take hold of the ship, they inquired if they might come on board, and upon permission being granted, they sprang up the side and shook every officer by the hand with undisguised feelings of gratification. The activity of the young men exceeded that of old Adams, who was consequently almost the last to greet us. He was in his sixty-fifth year, and was unusually strong and active for his age, notwithstanding the inconvenience of considerable corpulency. He was dressed in a sailor's shirt and trousers and a low-crowned hat, which he instinctively held in his hand until desired to put it on. He still retained his sailor's gait, doffing his hat and smoothing down his bald forehead whenever he was addressed by the officers. It was the first time he had been on board a ship of war since the mutiny, and his mind naturally reverted to scenes that could not fail to produce a temporary embarrassment, heightened, perhaps, by the familiarity with which he found himself addressed by persons of a class with those whom he had been accustomed to obey. Apprehension for his safety formed no part of his thoughts: he had received too many demonstrations of the good feeling that existed towards him, both on the part of the British government and of individuals, to entertain any alarm on that head; and as every person endeavored to set his mind at rest, he very soon made himself at home.

"The young men, ten in number, were tall, robust, and healthy, with good-natured countenances, which would any where have procured them a friendly reception; and with a simplicity of manner and a fear of doing wrong, which at once prevented the possibility of giving offence. Unacquainted with the world, they asked a number of questions which would have applied better to persons with whom they had been intimate, and who had left them but a short time before, than to perfect strangers: and inquired after ships and people we had never heard of. Their dress, made up of the presents which had been given them by the masters and seamen of ships, was a perfect caricature. Some had on long black coats without any other article of dress except trousers, some shirts without coats, and others waistcoats without either; none had shoes or stockings, and only two possessed hats, neither of which seemed likely to hang long together.

"The Blossom was so different, or, to use the expression of our visiters, 'so rich,' compared with the other ships they had seen, (it was so long since the visit of the Briton and Tagus that they had forgotten their appearance,) that they were constantly afraid of giving or committing some injury, and would not even move without first asking permission. This diffidence gave us full occupation for some time, as our restless visiters, anxious to see everything, seldom directed their attention long to any particular object, or remained in one position or place. Having no latches to their doors, they were ignorant of the manner of opening ours; and we were constantly attacked on all sides with 'Please may I sit down or get up, or go out of the cabin?' or, 'Please to open or shut the door.' Their applications were, however, made with such good nature and simplicity that it was impossible not to feel the greatest pleasure in paying attention to them. They very soon learnt the christian name of every officer in the ship, which they always used in conversation instead of the surname, and wherever a similarity to their own occurred, they attached themselves to that person as a matter of course.

"It was many hours after they came on board before the ship could get near the island, during which time they so ingratiated themselves with us that we felt the greatest desire to visit their houses; and rather than pass another night at sea we put off in the boats, though at a considerable distance from the land, and accompanied them to the shore. We followed our guides past a rugged point surmounted by tall spiral rocks, known to the islanders as St. Paul's rocks, into a spacious iron-bound bay, where the Bounty found her last anchorage. In this bay, which is bounded by lofty cliffs almost inaccessible, it was proposed to land. Thickly branched evergreens skirt the base of these hills, and in summer afford a welcome retreat from the rays of an almost vertical sun. In the distance are seen several high pointed rocks, which the pious highlanders have named after the most zealous of the Apostles, and outside of them is a square basaltic islet. Formidable breakers fringe the coast, and seem to present an insurmountable barrier to all access.

"We here brought our boats to an anchor, in consequence of the passage between the sunken rocks being much too intricate, and we trusted ourselves to the natives, who landed us, two at a time, in their whale boat. The difficulty of landing was more than repaid by the friendly reception we met with on the beach from Hannah Young, a very interesting young woman, the daughter of Adams. In her eagerness to greet her father, she had outrun her female companions, for whose delay she thought it necessary in the first place to apologize, by saying they had all been over the hill in company with John Buffett to look at the ship, and were not yet returned. It appeared that John Buffett, who was a seafaring man, ascertained that the ship was a man-of-war, and, without knowing exactly why, became so alarmed for the safety of Adams that he either could not or would not answer any of the interrogations which were put to him. This mysterious silence set all the party in tears, as they feared he had discovered something adverse to their patriarch. At length his obduracy yielded to their entreaties; but before he explained the cause of his conduct, the boats were seen to put off from the ship, and Hannah immediately hurried to the beach to kiss the old man's cheek, which she did with a fervency demonstrative of the warmest affection. Her apology for her companions was rendered unnecessary by their appearance on the steep and circuitous path down the mountain, who, as they arrived on the beach, successively welcomed us to their island, with a simplicity and sincerity which left no doubt of the truth of their professions.

"They almost all wore the cloth of the island: their dress consisted of a petticoat, and a mantle loosely thrown over the shoulders, and reaching to the ankles. Their stature was rather above the common height; and their limbs from being accustomed to work and climb the hills, had acquired unusual muscularity; but their features and manners were perfectly feminine. Their complexion, though fairer than that of the men, was of a dark gipsey hue, but its deep color was less conspicuous, by being contrasted with dark glossy hair, which hung down over the shoulders in long waving tresses, nicely oiled: in front it was tastefully turned back from the forehead and temples, and was retained in that position by a chaplet of small red or white aromatic blossoms, newly gathered from the flower-tree (*morinda citrifolia*), or from the tobacco plant; their countenances were lively and good natured, their eyes dark and animated, and each possessed an enviable row of teeth. Such was the agreeable impression of their first appearance, which was heightened by the wish expressed simultaneously by the whole group, that we were come to stay several days with them. As the sun was going down, we signified our desire to get to the village and to pitch the observatory before dark, and this was no sooner made known than every instrument and article found a carrier.

"We took the only pathway that leads from the landing-place

to the village, and soon experienced the difficulties of the ascent, which the distant appearance of the ground led us to anticipate. To the natives, however, there appeared to be no obstacles: women as well as men bore their burthens over the most difficult parts without inconvenience; while we, obliged at times to have recourse to tufts of shrubs or grass for assistance, experienced serious delay, being also incommoded by the heat of the weather, and by swarms of house-flies which infest the island, and are said to have been imported there by H. M. S. Briton. As soon as we had gained the first level, our party rested on some large stones that lay half buried in long grass on one side of a ravine, from which the blue sky was nearly concealed by the overlapping branches of palm-trees. Here, through the medium of our female guides, who, furnished with the spreading leaves of the tee-plant, drove away our troublesome persecutors we obtained a respite from their attacks.

"Having refreshed ourselves, we resumed our journey over a more easy path; and after crossing two valleys, shaded by cocoanut trees, we arrived at the village. It consisted of five houses, built upon a cleared piece of ground sloping to the sea, and commanding a distant view of the horizon, through a break in an extensive wood of palms. While the men assisted to pitch our tent, the women employed themselves in preparing our dinner, or, more properly, supper, as it was eight o'clock at night. The manner of cooking in Pitcairn's Island is similar to that of Tahiti, which, as some of my readers may not recollect, I shall briefly describe. An oven is made in the ground, sufficiently large to contain a good-sized pig, and is lined throughout with stones nearly equal in size, which have been previously made as hot as possible. These are covered with some broad leaves, generally of the tee-plant, and on them is placed the meat. If it be a pig, its inside is lined with heated stones, as well as the oven; such vegetables as are to be cooked are then placed round the animal: the whole is carefully covered with leaves of the tee, and buried beneath a heap of earth, straw, or rushes and boughs, which, by a little use, becomes matted into one mass. In about an hour and a quarter the animal is sufficiently cooked, and is certainly more thoroughly done than it would be by a fire.

"By the time the tent was up and the instruments secured, we were summoned to a meal cooked in this manner, than which a less sumptuous fare would have satisfied appetites rendered keen by long abstinence and a tiresome journey. Our party divided themselves that they might not crowd one house in particular: Adams did not entertain; but at Christian's I found a table spread with plates, knives, and forks; which, in so remote a part of the world, was an unexpected sight. They were, it is true, far from uniform; but by one article being appropriated for another, we all found something to put our portion upon; and but few of the natives were obliged to substitute their fingers for articles which are indispensable to the comfort of more polished life. The smoking pig, by a skillful dissection, was soon portioned to every guest, but no one ventured to put its excellent qualities to the test until a lengthened *Amen*, pronounced by all the party, had succeeded the imploring of a blessing, by the village parson [*John Buffett*]. In Pitcairn's Island it is not deemed proper to touch even a bit of bread without a grace before and after it, and a person is accused of inconsistency if he leaves off and begins again. So strict is their observance of this form, that we do not know of any instance in which it has been forgotten.

"Welcome cheer, hospitality, and good humor, were the characteristics of the feast; and never was their beneficial influence more practically exemplified than on this occasion, by the demolition of nearly all that was placed before us. With the exception of some wine we had brought with us, water was the only beverage. This was placed in a large jug at one end of the board, and, when necessary, was passed round the table —a ceremony at which, in Pitcairn's Island in particular, it is desirable to be the first partaker, as the gravy of the dish is invariably mingled with the contents of the pitcher; the natives, who prefer using their fingers to forks, being quite indifferent whether they hold the vessel by the handle or by the spout. Three or four torches made with doodoe nuts (*aleurites triloba*), strung upon the fibres of a palm-leaf, were stuck in tin pots at the end of the table, and formed an excellent substitute for candles, except that they gave a considerable heat, and cracked, and fired, somewhat to the discomfiture of the person whose face was near them. Notwithstanding these deficiencies, we made a very comfortable and hearty supper, heard many little anecdotes of the place, and derived much amusement from the singularity of the inquiries of our hosts. One regret only intruded itself upon the general conviviality, which we did not fail to mention, namely, that there was so wide a distinction between the sexes. This was the remains of a custom very common among the South Sea Islands, which in some places is carried to such an extent, that it imposes death upon the woman who shall eat in the presence of her husband; and though the distinction between man and wife is not here carried to that extent, it is still sufficiently observed to exclude all the women from table, if there happens to be a deficiency of seats. In Pitcairn's Island, they have settled ideas of right and wrong, to which they obstinately adhere; and, fortunately, they have imbibed them generally from the best source. In the instance in question, they have, however, certainly erred; but of this they could not be persuaded, nor did they, I believe, thank us for our interference. Their argument was, that man was made first, and ought, consequently, on all occasions, to be served first—a conclusion which deprived us of the company of the women at table, during the whole of our stay at the island. Far from considering themselves neglected, they very good-naturedly chatted with us behind our seats, and flapped away the flies, and by a gentle tap, accidentally or playfully delivered, reminded us occasionally of the honor that was done us. The conclusion of our meal was the signal for the women and children to prepare their own, to whom we resigned our seats, and strolled out to enjoy the freshness of the night.

"It was late by the time the women had finished, and we were not sorry when we were shown to the beds prepared for us. The mattress was composed of palm-trees, covered with native cloth; the sheets were of the same material; and we knew by the crackling of them, that they were quite new from the loom or beater. The whole arrangement was extremely comfortable, and highly inviting to repose, which the freshness of the apartment, rendered cool by a free circulation of air through its sides, enabled us to enjoy without any annoyance from heat or insects. One interruption only disturbed our first sleep; it was a pleasing melody of the evening hymn, which, after the lights were put out, was chanted by the whole family in the middle of the room. In the morning also we were awoke by their morning hymn and family devotion. As we were much tired, and the sun's rays had not yet found their way through the broad opening of the apartment, we composed ourselves to rest again; and on awaking found that all the natives were gone to their several occupations,—the men to offer what assistance they could to our boats in landing, carrying burthens for the seamen, or to gather what fruits were in season. Some of the women had taken our linen to wash; those whose turn it was to cook for the day were preparing the oven, the pig, and the yams; and we could hear, by the distant reiterated strokes of the beater, that others were engaged in the manufacture of cloth. By our bedside had already been placed some ripe fruits: and our hats were crowned with chaplets of the fresh blossom of the nono, or flower-tree (*morinda citrifolia*), which the women had gathered in the freshness of the morning dew. On looking round the apartment, though it contained several beds, we found no partition, curtain, or screens; they had not yet been considered necessary. So far, indeed, from concealment being thought of when we were about to get up, the women, anxious to show their attention, assembled to wish us a good morning, and to inquire in what way they could best contribute to our comforts, and to present us with some little gift, which the produce of the island afforded.

"We assembled at breakfast about noon, the usual eating hour of the natives, though they do not confine themselves to that period exactly, but take their meal whenever it is sufficiently cooked; and afterwards availed ourselves of their proffered services to show us the island, and under their guidance first inspected the village, and what lay in its immediate vicinity. In an adjoining house we found two young girls seated upon the ground, employed in the laborious exercise of beating out the bark of the cloth-tree, which they intended to present to us, on our departure, as a keepsake. The hamlet consisted of five cottages, built more substantially than neatly, upon a cleared patch of ground, sloping to the northward, from the high land of the interior to the cliffs which overhang the sea, of which the houses command a distant view in a northern direction. In the N. E. quarter, the horizon may also be seen peeping between the stems of the lofty palms, whose graceful branches nod like ostrich plumes to the refreshing trade-wind. To the northward, and northwestward, thicker groves of palm-trees rise in an impenetrable wood, from two ravines which traverse the hills in various directions to their summit. Above the one, to the westward, a lofty mountain rears its head, and towards the sea terminates in a fearful precipice filled with caverns, in which the different sea-fowl find an undisturbed retreat. Immediately round the village are the small enclosures for fattening pigs, goats, and poultry; and beyond them, the cultivated grounds producing the banana, plantain, melon, yam, taro, sweet potatoes, appai, tee, and cloth plant, with other useful roots, fruits, and shrubs, which extend far up the mountain and to the southward; but in this particular direction they are excluded from the view by an immense banyan tree, two hundred paces in circumference, whose foliage and branches form of themselves a canopy impervious to the rays of the sun. Every cottage has its out-house for making cloth, its baking-place, its sty, and its poultry-house.

"Within the enclosure of palm-trees is the cemetery where the few persons who had died on the island, together with those who met with violent deaths, are deposited. Besides the houses above mentioned, there are three or four others built upon the plantations beyond the palm groves. One of these, situated higher up the hill than the village, belonged to Adams, who had retired from the bustle of the hamlet to a more quiet and sequestered spot, to enjoy the advantages of an elevated situation, so desirable in warm countries; and in addition to these again there are four other cottages to the eastward which belong to the Youngs and Quintals. [A view of Adams's house, drawn by Beechey, is given on page 121.]

"All these cottages are strongly built of wood in an oblong form, and thatched with the leaves of the palm-tree bent round the stem of the same branch, and laced horizontally to rafters, so placed as to give a proper pitch to the roof. The greater part have an upper story, which is appropriated to sleeping, and contain four beds built in the angles of the room, each sufficiently large for three or four persons to lie on. They are made of

View of Aleck's Residence.

11

wood of the cloth-tree, and are raised eighteen inches above the floor; a mattress of palm-leaves is laid upon the planks, and above it three sheets of the cloth-plant, which form an excellent substitute for linen. The lower room generally contains one or more beds, but is always used as their eating-room, and has a broad table in one part, with several stools placed round it. The floor is elevated above a foot from the ground, and, as well as the sides of the house, is made of stout plank. The floor is a fixture, but the sideboards are let into a groove in the supporters, and can be removed at pleasure, according to the state of the weather, and the whole side may, if required, be laid open. The lower room communicates with the upper by a stout ladder in the centre, and leads up through a trap-door into the bedroom.

"From the village several pathways (for roads there are none) diverge, and generally lead into the valleys, which afford a less difficult ascent to the upper part of the island than the natural slope of the hills; still they are very rugged and steep, and in the rainy season so slippery that it is almost impossible for any person, excepting the natives, to traverse them with safety. We selected one which led over the mountain to the landing-place, on the opposite side of the island, and visited the several plantations upon the higher grounds, which extend towards the mountain with a gentle slope. Here the mutineers originally built their summer-houses, for the purpose of enjoying the breeze and overlooking the yam grounds, which are more productive than those lower down. Near these plantations are the remains of some ancient morais; and a spot is pointed out as the place where Christian was first buried. By a circuitous, and, to us, difficult path, we reached the ridge of the mountain, the height of which is 1109 feet above the sea; this is the highest part of the island. The ridge extends in a north and south direction, and unites two small peaks: it is so narrow as to be in many parts scarcely three feet wide, and forms a dangerous pass between two fearful precipices. The natives were so accustomed to climb these crags that they unconcernedly skipped from point to point like the hunters of chamois; and young Christian actually jumped upon the very peak of a cliff, which was so small as to be scarcely sufficient for his feet to rest upon, and from which any other person would have shuddered even to look down upon the beach, lying many hundred feet at its base. At the northern extremity of this ridge is a cave of some interest, as being the intended retreat of Christian, in the event of a landing being effected by any ship sent in pursuit of him, and where he resolved to sell his life as dearly as he could. In this recess he always kept a store of provisions, and near it erected a small hut, well concealed by trees, which served the purpose of a watchhouse. So difficult was the approach to this cave, that even if the party were successful in crossing the ridge, as long as his ammunition lasted, he might have bid defiance to any force. An unfrequented and dangerous path leads from this place to a peak which commands a view of the western and southern coasts: at this height, on a clear day, a perfect map of the bottom is exhibited by the different colored waters. On all points the island is terminated by cliffs, or rocky projections, off which lie scattered numerous fragments of rocks, rising like so many black pinnacles amid the surf, which on all sides rolls in upon the shore.

"We descended by a less abrupt slope than that by which we advanced, and took our way through yam grounds to a ravine which brought us to the village. The path leading down this ravine is, in many places, so precipitous, that we were constantly in danger of slipping and rolling into the depths below, which the assistance of the natives alone prevented. While we were thus borrowing help from others, and grasping every tuft of grass and bough that offered its friendly support, we were overtaken by a group of chubby little children, trudging unconcernedly on, munching a water melon, and balancing on their heads calabashes of water, which they had brought from the opposite side of the island. They smiled at our helplessness as they passed, and we felt their innocent reproof: but we were still unpractised in such feats, while they, from being trained to them, had acquired a footing and a firmness which habit alone can produce.

"It was dark when we reached the houses, but we found by a whoop which echoed through the woods, that we were not the last from home. This whoop, peculiar to the place, is so shrill, that it may be heard half over the island, and the ear of the natives is so quick, that they will catch it when we could distinguish nothing of the kind. By the tone in which it is delivered, they also know the wants of the person, and who it is. These shrill sounds, which we had just heard, informed us, and those who were at the village, that a party had lost their way in the woods. A blazing beacon was immediately made, which, together with a few more whoops to direct the party, soon brought the absentees home. Their perfection in these signals will be manifest from the following anecdote: I was one day crossing the mountain which intersects the island, with Christian; we had not long parted with their whale-boat on the western side of the island, and were descending a ravine amidst a thicket of trees, when he turned round and said, 'The whale-boat is come round to Bounty Bay;' at which I was not a little surprised, as I had heard nothing, and we could not see through the wood; but he heard the signal; and when we got down it proved to be the case.

"The following day was devoted to the completion of our view of the island, of which the natives were anxious we should see every part. We accordingly set out with the same guides by a road which brought us to 'the Rope,' a steep cliff so called from its being necessary to descend it by a rope. It is situated at the eastern end of the island, and overlooks a small sandy bay lined with rocks, which render it dangerous for a boat to attempt to land there. At the foot of 'the Rope' were found some stone axes, and a hone, the manufacture of the aborigines, and upon the face of a large rock were some characters very rudely engraved, which we copied; they appeared to have been executed by the Bounty's people, though Adams did not recollect it. To the left of 'the Rope' is a peak of considerable height, overlooking Bounty Bay. Upon this eminence the mutineers, on their arrival, found four images, about six feet in height, placed upon a platform; and, according to Adams's description, not unlike the morais at Easter Island, excepting that they were upon a much smaller scale. One of these images, which had been preserved, was a rude representation of the human figure to the hips, and was hewn out of a piece of red lava.

"Having this day seen every part of the island, we had no further desire to ramble; and as the weather did not promise to be very fair, I left the observatory in the charge of Mr. Wolfe, and embarked, accompanied by old Adams. Soon after he came on board it began to blow, and for several days afterwards the winds prevented any communication with the shore. The natives during this period were in great apprehension: they went to the top of the island every morning to look for the ship; and once, when she was not to be seen, began to entertain the most serious doubts whether Adams would be returned to them; but he, knowing we should close the island as soon as the weather would permit, was rather glad of the opportunity of remaining on board, and of again associating with his countrymen.

"On the 16th the weather permitted a boat to be sent on shore, and Adams was restored to his anxious friends. Previous to quitting the ship, he said it would add much to his happiness if I would read the marriage ceremony to him and his wife, as he could not bear the idea of living with her without its being done. He had long wished for the arrival of a ship of war to set his conscience at rest on that point. Though Adams was aged, and the old woman had been blind and bedridden for several years, he made such a point of it, that it would have been cruel to refuse him. They were accordingly the next day duly united, and the event noted in a register by John Buffet.

"The islanders were delighted at having us again among them, and expressed themselves in the warmest terms. We soon found, through our intercourse with these excellent people, that they had no wants excepting such as had been created by an intercourse with vessels, which have from time to time supplied them with European articles. Nature has been extremely bountiful to them; and necessity has taught them how to apply her gifts to their own particular uses. Still they have before them the prospect of an increasing population, with limited means of supporting it. Almost every part of the island capable of cultivation has been turned to account; but what would have been the consequences of this increase, had not an accident discovered their situation, it is not difficult to foresee: and a reflecting mind will naturally trace in that disclosure the benign interference of the same hand which has raised such a virtuous colony from so guilty a stock.

"During the period we remained upon the island we were entertained at the board of the natives; sometimes dining with one person, and sometimes with another: their meals, as I have before stated, were not confined to hours, and always consisted of baked pig, yams, and taro, and more rarely of sweet potatoes.

"The productions of the island being very limited, and intercourse with the rest of the world much restricted, it may be readily supposed their meals cannot be greatly varied. However, they do their best with what they have, and cook it in different ways, the pig excepted, which is always baked. There are several goats upon the island, but they dislike their flesh as well as their milk. Yams constitute their principal food; these are boiled, baked, or made into pillihey, (cakes,) by being mixed with cocoanuts; or bruised and formed into a soup. Bananas are mashed, and made into pancakes, or, like the yam, united with the milk of the cocoanut, into pillihey, and eaten with molasses extracted from the tee-root. The taro root, by being rubbed, makes a very good substitute for bread, as well as the bananas, plantain, and appai. Their common beverage is pure water, but they made for us a tea, extracted from the tee-plant, flavored with ginger, and sweetened with the juice of the sugar-cane. When alone, this beverage and fowl soup are used only for such as are ill. They seldom kill a pig, but live mostly upon fruit and vegetables. The duty of saying grace was performed by John Buffet, a recent settler among them, and their clergyman; but if he was not present, it fell upon the eldest of the company. They have all a great dislike to spirits, in consequence of M'Koy having killed himself by too free an indulgence in it; but wine, in moderation, is never refused. With this simple diet, and being in the daily habit of rising early, and taking a great deal of exercise in the cultivation of their grounds, it was not surprising that we found them so athletic and free from complaints. When illness does occur, their remedies are as simple as their manner of living, and are limited to salt water, hot ginger tea, or abstinence, according to the nature of the complaint. They have no medicines, nor do they appear to require any, as these remedies have hitherto been found sufficient.

"After their noontide meal, if their grounds do not require their attention, and the weather be fine, they go a little way out to sea in their canoes, and catch fish, of which they have several kinds, large and sometimes in abundance: but it seldom happens that they have this time to spare; for the cultivation of the ground, repairing their boats, houses, and making fishing-lines, with other employments, generally occupy the whole of each day. At sunset they assemble at prayers as before, first offering their orison and thanksgiving, and then chanting hymns. After this follows their evening meal, and at an early hour, having again said their prayers, and chanted the evening hymn, they retire to rest; but before they sleep, each person again offers up a short prayer upon his bed.

"Such is the distribution of time among the grown people; the younger part attend at school at regular hours, and are instructed in reading, writing, and arithmetic. They have very fortunately found an able and willing master in John Buffet, who, in addition to the instruction of the children, has taken upon himself the duty of clergyman, and is the oracle of the community. Another seaman has settled amongst them, and is married to one of Adams's daughters; but he is not liked. During the whole time I was with them I never heard them indulge in a joke, or other levity, and the practice of it is apt to give offence: they are so accustomed to take what is said in its literal meaning, that irony was always considered a falsehood in spite of explanation. They could not see the propriety of uttering what was not strictly true for any purpose whatever.

"The Sabbath-day is devoted entirely to prayer, reading, and serious meditation. No boat is allowed to quit the shore, nor any work whatever to be done, cooking excepted, for which preparation is made the preceding evening. I attended their church on this day, and found the service well conducted; the prayers were read by Adams, and the lessons by Buffet, the service being preceded by hymns. The greatest devotion was apparent in every individual, and in the children there was a seriousness unknown in the younger part of our communities at home. In the course of the Litany they prayed for their sovereign and royal family with much apparent loyalty and sincerity. Some family prayers, which were thought appropriate to their particular case, were added to the usual service; and Adams, fearful of leaving out any essential part, read, in addition, all those prayers which are intended only as substitutes for others. A sermon followed, which was very well delivered by Buffet; and lest any part of it should be forgotten or escape attention, it was read three times. The whole concluded with hymns, which were first sung by the grown people, and afterwards by the children. The service thus performed was very long; but the neat and cleanly appearance of the congregation, the devotion that animated every countenance, and the innocence and simplicity of the little children, prevented the attendance from becoming wearisome. In about half an hour afterwards we again assembled to prayers, and at sunset service was repeated; so that, with their morning and evening prayers, they may be said to have church five times on Sunday.

"Marriages and christenings are duly performed by Adams. A ring which has united every person on the island is used for the occasion, and given according to the prescribed form. The age at which this is allowed to take place, with the men, is after they have reached their twentieth, and with the women, their eighteenth year.

"All which remains to be said of these excellent people is, that they appear to live together in perfect harmony and contentment; to be virtuous, religious, cheerful, and hospitable beyond the limits of prudence; to be patterns of conjugal and parental affection, and to have very few vices. We remained with them many days, and their unreserved manners gave us the fullest opportunity of becoming acquainted with any faults they might have possessed.

"In return for the kindness we experienced from the islanders, we made them presents of articles the most useful to them which we could spare, and they were furnished with a blue cloth suit each from the extra clothing put on board for the ship's company, and the women with several pieces of gowns and handkerchiefs, &c. When we were about to take leave, our friends assembled to express their regret at our departure. All brought some little present for our acceptance, which they wished us to keep in remembrance of them; after which they accompanied us to the beach, where we took our leave of the female part of the inhabitants. Adams and the young men pushed off in their own boat to the ship, determined to accompany us to sea as far as they could with safety. They continued on board, unwilling to leave us, until we were a considerable distance from land, when they shook each of us feelingly by the hand, and, amidst expressions of the deepest concern at our departure, wished us a prosperous voyage, and hoped that we might one day meet again. As soon as they were clear of the ship, they all stood up in the boat, and gave us three hearty cheers, which were as heartily returned. As the weather became foggy, the barge towed them towards the shore, and we took a final leave of them, unconscious until the moment of separation of the warm interest their situation and good conduct had created in us."

The life of Aleck was prolonged somewhat more than three years after this visit of the ship Blossom. A letter, received from the island by Captain Beechey, some time after he had returned to England, gave information that John Adams died in March, 1829, being about seventy years old. It was an unspeakable loss to the colony to be deprived of their venerable patriarch. His likeness, with a fac-simile of his hand-writing, as published by Captain Beechey, is given on page 129.

Before his death, being anxious lest, after his departure, there should be strife among them, he called all the heads of families together and advised them to appoint a chief, or ruler, to take his place. This proposal was not relished by the young men; they answered,—"Father, we are willing to obey you as long as you live; but when you are gone, we shall be all alike." It has been reported that he wished them to choose as his successor, his own son, George Adams; but an American captain, whose visit to this island will be noticed in a subsequent chapter, says that he never heard the people mention this, although in his opinion George was the most suitable person among them to be their governor. On the approach of death, Adams manifested entire resignation to the will of God, and begged his people all to serve the Lord faithfully, to "obey that God who had made them his children through the merits of Christ Jesus."

Previously to his death, a code of laws had been drawn up, which was signed by John Adams and seven others who were, at the time of signing, the only married men; and every head of a family was to sign the same as soon as married, and promise not to favor his own children if ever found to be transgressors.

In the course of the five years immediately subsequent to Captain Beechey's visit, some American vessels, from Nantucket, on whaling voyages, touched at Pitcairn's; but the next information of special interest was obtained through Captain Waldegrave, who arrived at the island in March, 1830, commander of the British ship Seringapatam. This vessel was sent, in consequence of representations made by Captain Beechey respecting the wants of the islanders, to carry out to them from the British government, certain supplies, including a pro-

John Adams.

I

portion for sixty persons of the following articles: sailors' blue jackets and trousers, flannel waistcoats, pairs of stockings and shoes, women's dresses, spades, mattocks, shovels, pickaxes, trowels, rakes.

The ship had scarcely anchored when George Young was alongside in his canoe, which he guided by a paddle; and soon after Thursday October Christian, in a jolly-boat, with several others, who, having come on board, were invited to breakfast, and one of them said grace as usual both before and after it. The captain, the chaplain, and some other officers accompanied these natives on shore, and having reached the summit of the first level or plain, which is surrounded by a grove or screen of cocoanut-trees, they found the wives and mothers assembled to receive them. "I have brought you a clergyman," says the captain.—"God bless you," issued from every mouth; "but is he come to stay with us?"—"No."—"You bad man, why not?"—"I cannot spare him, he is the chaplain of my ship; but I have brought you clothes and other articles, which King George has sent you."—"But," says Kitty Quintal, "we want food for our souls."

"Our reception," says Captain Waldegrave, "was most cordial, particularly that of Mr. Watson, the chaplain; and the meeting of the wives and husbands most affecting, exchanging expressions of joy that could not have been exceeded had they just returned from a long absence. The men sprang up to the trees, throwing down cocoanuts, the husks of which were torn off by others with their teeth, and offering us the milk. As soon as we had rested ourselves, they took us to their cottages, where we dined and slept."

Captain Waldegrave says it was highly gratifying to observe their native simplicity of manners, apparently without guile; their hospitality was unbounded, their cottages being open to all, and all were welcome to such food as they possessed; pigs and fowls were immediately killed and dressed, and when the guests were seated, one of the islanders, in the attitude of prayer, and his eyes raised towards heaven, repeated a simple grace for the present food they were about to partake of, beseeching, at the same time, spiritual nourishment; at the end of which each responded *Amen*. On the arrival of any one during the repast, they all paused until the new guest had said grace.

At night they all assembled in one of the cottages to hear the afternoon church service performed by Mr. Watson, and Captain Waldegrave describes it as a most striking scene. The place chosen was the bedroom of one of the double cottages, or one with an upper story. The ascent was by a broad ladder from the lower room through a trap-door. The clergyman took his station between two beds, with a lamp burning close behind him. In the bed on his right were three infants sound asleep; at the foot of that on his left were three men sitting. On each side and in front were the men, some wearing only the simple mara, displaying their gigantic figures; others in jackets and trousers, their necks and feet bare; behind stood the women, in their modest home-made cloth dresses, which entirely covered the form, leaving only the head and feet bare. The girls wore, in addition, a sheet knotted in the manner of a Roman senator's *toga*, thrown over the right shoulder and under the left arm. When the general confession commenced, they all knelt down facing the clergyman, with their hands raised to their breast in the attitude of prayer, slowly and distinctly repeating the confession after the clergyman. They prayed for the king of England, whom they consider as their sovereign. A sermon followed, from a text which Captain Waldegrave thinks was most happily chosen: "Fear not, little flock, for it is your Father's good pleasure to give you the kingdom." At the conclusion of the service they requested permission to sing their parting hymn, when the whole congregation, in good time, sang, "Depart in peace."

Captain Waldegrave, like all former visitors, bears testimony to the kind disposition and active benevolence of these simple islanders. The children, he says, are fond and obedient, the parents affectionate and kind towards their children. None of the party ever heard a harsh word made use of by one towards another. They never slander or speak ill of one another. If any question was asked as to the character or conduct of a particular individual, the answer would probably be something of this kind, "If it could do any good, I would answer you; but as it cannot, it would be wrong to tell tales;" or if the question applied to one who had committed a fault, they would say, "It would be wrong to tell my neighbor's shame." The kind and benevolent feeling of these amiable people is extended to the surviving widows of the Tahiti men who were slain on the island; as they would be left in a helpless and destitute state, were it not for the humane consideration of the younger part of the society, by whom they are supported and regarded with every mark of attention.

CHAPTER XI.

THE REMOVALS.

"Seats of my youth, when every sport could please!
Dear lovely bowers of innocence and ease!
This heart yet clings to thee, my native green,
Where humble happiness endear'd each scene."

When Aleck, in his old age, looked upon his growing family, and contemplated their probable increase in future years, it was very natural to feel some anxiety lest the means of support on so small an island should ere long prove insufficient. He expressed his fears to Captain Beechey, and requested him to ask the attention of the British government to the subject. In consequence of this, that government determined to take measures for removing the whole population to some other place. Mr. Nott, one of the missionaries stationed at Tahiti, being in England at the time, and being solicited to give his opinion respecting a suitable one, expressed himself in favor of Tahiti, and on his return to that island he was intrusted with a letter from Lord Bathurst to Pomare, requesting him, as king, to receive the colony from Pitcairn's Island under his protection. In an assembly of chiefs, in 1829, Pomare gave assurance to Captain Laws, commander of the Satellite, that he would welcome the Pitcairners, and allot them a tract of land. Meanwhile, before anything decisive as to their removal was effected, the British government, through the influence of Sir George Murray, in order to render their abode on their native island more comfortable, sent out the articles by Captain Waldegrave in the ship Seringapatam, as related in chapter tenth.

It would seem that the anxiety of Adams never ceased entirely. Not long before his death he addressed a letter to the government representing the necessity of a removal of the people. The Home Government

12

then ordered the authorities at New South Wales to provide means for effecting the object; and, accordingly, the sloop of war Comet, commanded by Captain Sandiland, accompanied by the transport Lucy Ann, was despatched from Sidney, in October, 1830. Captain Sandiland touched at New Zealand, and thence proceeded to Pitcairn's Island, where he arrived in February, 1831. According to some accounts, the inhabitants were very reluctant to leave their homes; but other accounts state, that as soon as informed that there was an opportunity to emigrate to Tahiti, one half immediately declared their determination to do so, and the remainder came to the same conclusion on the next day. They accordingly all embarked, and were conveyed safely to Tahiti, where the reigning Queen assigned them a tract of land. Here, however, they could not be contented. In less than a year, after much unhappiness and suffering, they effected their return to their own beloved island. The reader will receive an account of this portion of their history from the worthy and intelligent Captain William Driver, of Salem, Massachusetts, who conveyed them home from Tahiti in the brig Charles Doggett, and who, at my request, very kindly wrote a careful statement, which I shall give in his own words. But, in order that the reader may fully understand some of the allusions, it will be necessary to consider the state of things at Tahiti when the emigrants from Pitcairn's Island arrived.

The king, Pomare, mentioned in the first chapter, had been dead several years. He was succeeded by his son, Pomare III., a mere child, whose coronation took place when Messrs. Tyerman and Bennett were at the island on their tour to visit the various stations of the London Missionary Society; an account of the ceremonies may be found in their Journal. Pomare III. died in 1826, at the age of six years, and was succeeded by his sister Aimatta, then about sixteen years old. She was married to a young chief of Tahaa, to whom her father had (perhaps in consequence of the marriage,) given the royal name Pomare; but as he was a short corpulent person, the natives, in allusion to his figure, and in conformity with their usual custom, had added the appropriate but not very elegant surname of Aboo-rai, or Big-belly; he is the one who has just been mentioned as having promised, in 1829, a tract of land to the inhabitants of Pitcairn. For some reason the Queen seems about this time to have separated from her husband, who retired to the island Tahaa. In the beginning of the year 1831, some differences arose between the Queen and the hereditary chiefs; the dispute was at its height, and the hostile parties were just on the eve of a civil war, when Captain Sandiland arrived at Tahiti in the Comet. By his interposition, aided by the English missionaries, the differences were, however, soon amicably adjusted. From this officer's statement, it appears that the missionaries were held in great estimation both by the Queen and by the chiefs; yet it should here be remarked, that the influence of Christianity among the people had for some years been much less than under the reign of Pomare II.; iniquity and vice had gained great sway, to which the introduction and free use of ardent spirits had greatly contributed; and many native members of the church had been excommunicated for unchristian conduct. The following is the statement of Captain Driver.

"As early as the year 1829, or thereabouts, a letter was received by the British government, from John Adams, the then only survivor of the crew of the Bounty, in which he stated, that, should the people continue to increase as they had done, there would be a scarcity of water, and it would be necessary to remove them to some suitable place, to prevent their dying by drought; which, no doubt, occasioned the death of the former inhabitants of this little island, whose remains have frequently been found in caves, and some of whose tools I have in my possession, as a proof that it was once inhabited by a different race.

"In consequence of the above mentioned letter, in the commencement of the year 1831, a British sloop of war and a transport ship appeared off the island for the purpose of taking this then lovely little family to a place better suited to their wants. Who ther the contents of the above mentioned letter were known among the people I cannot say; yet certain it is, that the arrival of the ships was unexpected, and caused sorrow among the wiser part of the islanders, who have often told me that nothing but the arguments of one Mr. Henry, and a *scarcity of water*, which happened at the time, together with the entreaty of their children, could have induced them to consent to a removal. Say they, 'The tears of our children, drawn from them by the hope of seeing a land of "milk and honey," as described to them by Mr. Henry: these tears, and a wish to make them happy, led us to partake of the bitter cup of sorrow, by entering that world from which we had been so long and happily secluded.' After some dispute they all embarked on the first Sabbath in March, eighty-nine souls, among whom were two of the Tahitian women that accompanied the mutineers in the Bounty. Nothing worthy of note seems to have occurred during their passage of twenty-one days. I have seldom heard them speak except of the *tender feeling* and kindness of the commanders of that expedition; no swearing, lewdness, nor aught that could offend them, was allowed; and, say they, 'we really thought we had judged the world uncharitably in fearing its temptations.' They anchored at Toanoa road, in Tahiti, late in the evening of the last Sabbath in March; and their glad hearts leapt for joy to see the fruitful hills of that island, in all their native verdure, before them. Here, thought they, 'we shall have a home, situated in the very bosom of Eden! here, by the soft murmuring brook, we will chant those songs which once echoed among the black caverns of Pitcairn.' It was the Sabbath, and as no communication is held with vessels on that day, they remained on board, anxiously awaiting the morning's dawn. With that dawn came the shout of war. Along those very hills, in that Eden of yesterday, appeared hundreds, composing the Pomare (or Queen's) party, the very offscouring of *vice* and *depravity*, who had assembled for the express purpose of destroying the hopes of many Christians, and removing from the isle every vestige of virtue and religion. [If in this sentence the writer intended that the object of the Queen herself was to banish the missionaries and their religion, it is probably incorrect; many in her army, it is very likely, had such wishes, since, as above mentioned, there was at that time a great prevalence of vice among the Tahitians.] Happily for our Saviour's cause, the guns of the ships, together with the strength of the missionary party, had too formidable an appearance for these wretches.

"Such a scene, together with the circumstance of being on board of a man-of-war, whose decks now swarmed with women and men of the lowest character, from the shore, made an impression on the minds of this heretofore happy people never to be erased, and more easily conceived than described. With tearful eyes, pointing to their children, they begged to be taken from this sink of pollution back to their native hills; nothing would pacify them; nothing could banish from their minds the idea, that they should live to see their children borne down the tide of vice to eternal ruin! Virtuous to a proverb in their own isle, they looked with more than detestation on the *voluptuous* Tahitians. Their detestation was mingled with fear: such fear as must always accompany that virtue which has never been called to meet its foe. To see vice as they now did, all at once, in almost every shape that could shock them, was more than they could bear, and drove them almost to madness; this was the cause of all their sorrows. Time after time have I heard them tell their feelings on that horrid day, as they called it; and I know no reason to doubt their narrative.

"To take them back in the same vessels was impossible without an order from the British government, and they were landed at Toanoa, in Tahiti. The natives gave up to them most of the village of Bolyata, to dwell in until they could build and settle upon a tract of land assigned them by the Queen (Pomarè). The English government supplied them with provisions for six months, together with clothing, farming utensils, and every article which could conduce to their welfare, not omitting a fine library; yet, neither these things, nor

12*

aught else, could remove their first impressions, or lead them to think of anything but their forsaken isle! their dear home! Fearful and jealous of all around them, they became careless, indolent, and dirty, and huddled together like a flock of affrighted sheep. In this situation disease found them, and swept off twelve, the flower of their number, and left the rest in despair, the emaciated shadows of what they once were. Hope seemed to have fled, and a sort of sullen apathy appeared to fetter their souls, and to be fitting them for the snares which the votaries of vice had set around them. In vain did the worthy Mr. Pritchard and other missionaries talk to them of Israel's God and the Gentiles' Saviour. They were strangers in a strange land. In this condition I found them on my arrival; beset with evil, without a hope of change or rescue left save in death, they seemed a ready, helpless prey for the destroyer; and, no doubt, had they continued long in Tahiti, they would have lost that name for which they have been so admired, *the virtuous Pitcairners*.

"On my arrival, the latter part of July, 1831, this distressed people, one and all, urged me to take them home, offering to sell everything they possessed to pay the expenses. Finally, by means of a subscription among the missionaries, and selling some old copper and other articles, they obtained the sum requisite to defray the expenses of my vessel, and we embarked them on the 14th of August, 1831, sixty-five in number, twelve having started before in a small vessel. If ever joy was depicted in any face, it was in those of the Pitcairners as we swayed our sails aloft and filled away for that home from which they had been absent about six months. We arrived off their island late on Saturday, September 3d, after a smooth passage of twenty-one days, all well. At the shout of 'land, O!' some might be seen weeping over the clothing (which was all that remained) of their departed friends; others pacing the deck slowly; very few were willing to give way to joy. Poor fellows! as we drew near the land, a silent sorrow appeared to pervade the whole, and the universal feeling seemed to be—'We are now about to shut ourselves forever from the world.' One family (the McKoys) wanted to return.

"We finished landing them on Sunday, September 4th. I landed with them, and found on the island ten of the twelve that started in the other vessel, two having died. That day will, I trust, never be forgotten on the island, and certainly I never expect or wish to erase it from my mind. All else seemed forgotten, than the (to them painful) thought that we must be soon parted forever. They united and humbly besought God to bless us; we became women; we wept like children, until I extricated myself from them, and leaped into that boat which bore me forever from their shore. 'God bless you, we will write your name upon our walls,' was the last sound which caught my ear. Such is a sketch of one of the happiest occurrences in my life. If ever I knew, or shall know, the pleasure of blessing others, surely it was when I saw this people safe on their native shore, commencing anew their labors and devotion.

"During our passage up I was sorry to find many bad effects springing from their intercourse with the Tahitians. They seemed inclined to indolence, and to possess a good share of vanity and envy: traits which are too common among Tahitians, at least among those with whom I have been familiar. There was a want of sympathy and kindness between the families for which I could not account, and which often gave me pain. No doubt these passions were in part foreign, and I hope they will shake them off when left alone on their little island. The loose expressions of the Tahitians too often mingled with their common conversation, showing that their souls had inhaled the pollution, and of all their former devotion, I saw only the cold and lifeless remains, in forms and ceremonies. As they met around their daily food, before partaking there was a moving of the lips, as if to crave a blessing, but no audible sound nor voice, save in the last response, 'for Christ's sake;' such also was the sound as they retired to rest. I frequently addressed them alone on this subject, and spoke strongly on the necessity of brotherly love and union among them, but all seemed dull and cold, and often constrained me to say, 'Poor fellows, you have sad cause to remember Tahiti.'" In this condition of things, after their return to the home of their childhood, now rendered dearer to them by their absence for a time, Providence sent them a spiritual teacher. A Mr. George H. Nobbs, who had spent his early life at sea, and who seems to have been an energetic and excellent man, came among them, and was accepted by them as their spiritual guide. This man, of whom further mention is made in the concluding part of this book, has been represented as a "wolf in the fold;" but there is now good evidence that injustice has been done by these representations. The Islanders themselves have borne ample testimony to his good character and qualities; and, in view of this, the testimony of seamen who have casually visited the island is certainly to be received "with allowance." The commander of the ship who conveyed them back to their home in 1831 says:

"When we left them, they were seventy-five in number, generally young. They said they had enough of everything but water, for which they intended to blow a well. Their island, I think, is capable of supporting at least *one thousand*, provided they can obtain water, which at all times has been scarce, only oozing from the rocks, and often in so small quantities that the droppings of a night will barely meet the calls of the next day. Should they not succeed in obtaining water by blowing or some other means, I fear their whitened bones will some day bask unburied in the sun. I often told them so; and, in answer, they would say, 'Anything is better than Tahiti; and if we die here we shall sleep with our fathers, and at least have the consolation of having lost our lives by endeavoring to shun vice.'

"I will now endeavor to give you a faint idea of the general appearance of the island, the coast of which is a bold steep of rugged rocks, rising abruptly from the ocean to the height of at least two hundred feet, with scarcely a green shrub. I believe there are but two paths up to the region of vegetation, which is above, and forms a pleasing contrast with this brown base. As you approach the island from the westward, it appears well covered about the hill-tops and sides with wood; but on coming around to the north-western or south-eastern side, it appears a curious specimen of nature's works: you see here a dark brown heap of sterility, almost defying the footsteps of man; and there, a beautiful grove of ever-green, whose trees afford both food and raiment for the simple inhabitants. There are several groves of cocoas on the northern side, near the town. On the whole, I can sincerely say I never saw an island more pleasing to the eye. It is almost like a heap of rocks covered with everlasting green. [See the view of the island on page 11.]

"The coast being rocky and steep, we had much trouble in landing. A man sat upon a rock to watch the swell: when there was a favorable chance he waved a white cloth, and we gave way with all our oars so as to go in on the last roller; even then, with all our care, we often got a *dousing*, and endangered our boats. [A view of the landing at Bounty Bay is given on page 149.] The sea is generally so rough as to render it unsafe to anchor any where about the island. In 1830, a small schooner (employed as tender to a French brig in the pearl fishery,) anchored about ten rods northward of Bounty Bay, and in a few hours foundered at her anchors, the crew barely escaping with their lives.

"The town or village, consisting of about eleven houses, is situated on the northern (or north-northwestern) side of the island, on an elevated plain about three hundred feet above the ocean. It has a pleasing appearance from the sea on ship-board. Three of the largest houses stand in front, along the brow of a steep precipice, at the foot of which the ocean throws up its foam. The remainder of the houses are mingled romantically among a beautiful grove of cocoanut trees. Over these, in the back ground, rises a dark rugged heap of rocks here and there, nourishing a few hardy trees, but generally too barren to support anything, save the wild goat, which may be seen feeding or frolicking among the brown crags (called by the islanders the goat-pasture). I think, from Bounty Bay (or where the ship was lost,) to the town, is not over one third of a mile, in a west-northwesterly direction. The path is crooked, rough, and tiresome, as described by Beechey; yet, to a New-Englander, such a tramp is always pleasing, as it reminds him of the rugged features of his parent soil. From the town you have a fine view of the ocean, yet seldom see vessels until they double away the eastern point of the island, as the land hooks out in that direction, and thus, in part, forms what is called Bounty Bay. Off the point stand several rocks, called the St. Paul's. Over these the sea often dashes in a frightful manner, casting a spray at least eighty feet in air. There is a large rock also off the northern point, over which the sea often plunges when the wind is northward, although it is thirty or forty feet high. These rocks are so close to the island, that unless you are very near them they appear connected with it. Landing, always dangerous, is sometimes impossible for a month at a time. At these times, the inhabitants, being unable to go out a fishing, are obliged to live mostly on yams and other vegetables, and fruit. They have pigs and goats, but not enough to admit of killing often, and, of course, fish makes a great part of their food. In fair weather the islanders spend their Saturdays fishing on a bank, which extends some distance from the southern part of the island.

"There are now [that is when Captain Driver conveyed the people back to Tahiti,] five distinct families, viz., the Adamses, the Quintals, the Youngs, the Christians, and the McKoys; if you add to these the Englishmen, Evans, Buffett, and Nobbs, you have eight. The most active and intelligent of the natives are the *Adamses*, who inherit the characteristics of their father, that activity and decision which enabled him to leave behind him the name of *good father*—a name always used when speaking of him on the island. Next come the *Quintals*, who are darker, taller, and handsomer, than the Adamses, but have not their persevering industry or open generosity; they generally wear a look of content-

Landing in Bounty Bay.

ment and ease. Next to this family I should place the Youngs, who are a tall, lean, melancholy looking race. Their minds are of that unhappy cast which leads them to think lightly of their neighbors; but on the whole they have but little influence, on which account they are somewhat uneasy. The fourth family, the Christians, are mostly females. Their mother is living; the widow of Fletcher Christian. The only idiot on the island is Joseph Christian, a tall, stout, handsome, yet fierce-looking man, with a very dark complexion. He shuns strangers, and always appears grieved when any one looks hard at him. He is said to be very fond of being alone; often spending the whole day on some lonely cliff, with no other companion than his pipe and tobacco, of which he is very fond. One of the females of this family unhappily became a victim of seduction by an Englishman, before the removal to Tahiti; another lost her husband at Tahiti; and another is now married to Nobbs. Last of all we come to the M'Koys, who seem to be at ease any where, so long as they have peace and food. Perhaps the loss of a mother, a brother, and, I believe, two sisters, which took place at Tahiti, gives them a very dull appearance. This is the family that wanted to return to Tahiti.

"Their laws, I think, are extracts from the Mosaic; they relate principally to land trespasses and thefts; for the former the offender is whipped; for the latter, he restores three-fold. Seduction subjects the parties to eighty lashes each, and the female to contempt, and the male to banishment forever from the island in the first ship that will take him. Every head of a family, as soon as married, signs the laws, and swears not to favor even his own children should they transgress. The voice of two thirds of the people is necessary to sentence any one. As to the manner of conducting their trials, I am unacquainted. I believe they have not had a case since the laws were written. The case of seduction above alluded to was before, and was, no doubt, the occasion of having the present written laws, which are signed by old Adams and seven others, who at that time (1829) were married men."

Captain Driver adds, in conclusion, "Such is an impartial sketch of this people, as I saw them. But when you consider their loss of friends, their disappointments, and their sufferings,—when you remember that they went out, as it were, full, and now returned home empty, you will not wonder; but, I am convinced, will pity them, that their virtues seem to hang on the brink of a precipice, from which they may be hurled to everlasting ruin, unless some friendly arm is extended to save them."

Whoever has been much interested in perusing the above narrative and remarks, must be very desirous to know the course which things took among these families after their return, as it were, from captivity. In the next chapter I shall present to the reader all I have learned that is important.

CHAPTER XII.

THE SEQUEL.

"But chief my fear the dangers mov'd
That virtue's path enclose;
My heart the wise pursuit approv'd,
But, oh! what toils oppose!
For see, while yet in virtue's ways
With anxious step I tread,
A hostile world its terrors raise,
Its snares delusive spread."

How noble that feeling which the poor Pitcairnians expressed, when they signified their readiness to perish of thirst or famine, if they might only die in the possession of virtue, and lay their bones in the sepulchre of their fathers! But their circumstances, as described in the preceding chapter, were such, that they could not but find the path of virtue beset with new dangers, after their return to their native island. No wonder that every friend to their welfare looked with trembling solicitude for the sequel.

In the spring of the year 1837, Captain Bunker, from Falmouth, in Massachusetts, commander of a vessel voyaging in the Pacific ocean, touched at the island. The account given by him to a friend, from whom I received it, was as follows :—

"The island seems to have been a vast mass of rock, upon which the vegetation of successive years has accumulated a soil in some places several feet deep. In some portions it is very fertile; but the higher parts of the island are still naked rock. Captain Bunker sailed around it several times; it has no proper harbor, and a bad surf must always be encountered in landing. The number of the inhabitants was upwards of 90: most of them were able to read and write. Two women, who had been wives of the mutineers, were still living, being very aged. One of the men was represented to be the son of Christian, the instigator of the mutiny. The British government having proposed to the people to select some one to be their chief magistrate, or governor, they had chosen Edward Quintal for the purpose. He was the son of the mutineer Matthew Quintal, and was a discreet and intelligent man, about 42 years of age. A certain number of acres of ground was assigned for each family. Just before Captain Bunker was there, the islanders had received as a gratuity from the British government a new supply of clothing, with a fishing apparatus and other useful articles. But their moral state was not so good as it had formerly been. Intemperance had found its way among them. Although Adams had sent the old still from the island, [as mentioned on page 109,] two had been set up in its place, after his death; and there had been some quarrels and much bitterness.

But the next intelligence is more agreeable. It was obtained by Captain Emmons, of the ship Cyrus. He visited the island in the year 1839. His account was the following, as gathered from the newspaper entitled the Nantucket Inquirer :—

"The island contains about 100 inhabitants, who are a very moral and religious people. The services of religion are strictly regarded, and Mr. Emmons informs us that the worship he attended, though conducted in their school-house, was marked with such propriety and decorum as are rarely to be witnessed even in our own country.

"In this instance, as in every other, religious improvement and moral civilization have gone hand in hand together. The in habitants have houses built of wood, generally constructed like the cabin of a ship. In their other domestic habits they are industrious, decent, and orderly, and, grateful for the blessings they enjoy, are content and happy. They know nothing of religious feuds or political controversy; they live like brethren, '*in the unity of the spirit and in the bond of peace*,' having '*one Lord, one faith, one baptism, one God and Father of all, who is above all, and through all, and in all.*'

"Grateful for the hospitality which had been shown him, Captain Emmons ventured, on his departure, to tender some remuneration, but none would they accept; save in the form of *religious books!* Having a few of these in his possession, he gladly presented them; and he affirms that he was more than gratified to think that he had been able to contribute satisfactorily to the spiritual necessities of these kind people, who have a thirst for religious knowledge. So 'precious is the word of the Lord' unto them.

"We are indebted to Mr. Emmons for the copy of verses given below. Independently of their intrinsic merit, these stanzas will carry with them an interest, which any ordinary composition would not command, on account of the source from whence they originate. They are the productions of a young man, who, though not born in a country blessed, as is ours, with what are usually termed religious privileges, must yet have been a Christian indeed! The language is highly chaste and appropriate, scriptural, and full of piety; and no one can either gainsay the feelings which dictated or the manner in which the sentiments are expressed, for some of the verses are really beautiful. These verses are in the hand-writing of *a* John Adams, a lad of *eleven* years of age, whose proficiency in penmanship would well compare with that of boys of a similar age in any of our public schools,—which may therefore be regarded as a favorable index of the state of education in the island."

"THE WORDS OF MR. JOHN QUINTAL, JR.

"*On his dying bed, November* 21, 1838. *Pitcairn's Island.*

My sisters, my brethren, your sorrow restrain,
All human endeavors are futile and vain,
My hours are numbered, the summons is come,
I feel that this world is no longer my home,
Home, home, uncertain home,
I feel that this world is no longer my home.

"No terror I feel in the prospect of death,
The bright beams of hope gild the valley beneath,
By faith I perceive, through the clouds and the gloom,
That Jesus, in mercy, is calling me home.
Home, home, sweet, sweet home,
My Jesus, in mercy, is calling me home.

"What though my poor body convulsively start,
There is peace in the mind, there is joy in the heart,

Such strength for my days doth the Saviour supply.
My pains are as nothing—'t is nothing to die.
No, no, nothing to die,
Believe me, believe me, 't is nothing to die.

" Wife, children, and mother, farewell for a while,
That tear on your cheeks should give place to a smile,
If ye be found faithful, the time will soon come,
When Jesus will call you to meet me at home.
Home, home, sweet, sweet home,
My Jesus will call you to meet me at home.

" I thirst, but the water I languish to taste
Ye cannot procure me, in vain is your haste;
'T is the stream of Salvation, Immanuel's blood,
The water that gladdens the city of God.
Flow, flow, sweet, sweet flood,
And cleanse me, and bear me to Jesus my God.

" An angel! an angel! lo, yonder he stands,
In white robes arrayed, a crown in his hand;
He beckons me to him, he seems to say come,
I 'm waiting to crown you and carry you home
Home, home, sweet, sweet home,
'The Master' hath sent me to carry you home.

" Think not that disease has enfeebled my mind,
Nor deem it presumption to be thus resigned,
I know on whose promise, by faith, I believe,
I know he doth change not, He cannot deceive.
No, no, never deceive,
My Jesus he will not, he cannot deceive.

" In me there is nothing affection to win,
By nature and practice infected with sin,
No merits on which I dependence can place,
Eternal salvation is all of free grace.
Grace, grace, free, free grace,
'T is unbounded mercy, 't is love and free grace.

" My Saviour, I see him, in glory, how bright,
Though angels surround him and hinder my sight;
But when I arrive at the mansions of bliss,
I shall bow at his feet and him see as he is.
I? I? Yes; O yes,
I shall bow at his feet, and him see as he is.

" O strengthen me, Jesus, the conflict comes on,
And nature resists, though I fain would be gone;
The passage is rugged, yet still I can sing
Where, grave, is thy victory? Death, where 's thy sting?
Where? Where? Death 's thy sting?
Where, grave, is thy victory? Death, where 's thy sting?

" The struggle is over, receive my last breath—
Sustained by my Saviour, I triumph o'er death;

On Him, and Him only, I wholly rely;
Since he has redeemed me, 't is nothing to die.
No, no, nothing to die,
Believe me, believe me, 't is nothing to die.

" Our brother has left us, to join in the song
Of all the redeemed, the glorified throng,
And may we be ready to answer 'I come,'
Whene'er we are summoned to meet him at home.
Home, home, eternal home,
At Jesus' right hand may we meet him at home."

An intelligent and pious young man, who went out as a carpenter in a ship bound on a whaling voyage in the Pacific, and kept a journal of events, gives an interesting account of a visit at Pitcairn's Island. The ship arrived there July 18, 1839, and remained until near the first of August, for the purpose of obtaining supplies. During this time the presence of this young man was required on shore, where he enjoyed, in consequence, the best opportunities for observing the condition of this people; and he recorded the facts which passed under his notice for his own private satisfaction. The following extracts from his journal were published in the Christian Watchman.

" We were invited this evening to the house of Mr. B. [Buffett,] where we took lodgings. And let me say, that since leaving home I have not spent an evening more agreeably. Mr. B. has a wife and family of four children; the wife is daughter of Fletcher Christian, well known in history as the leader of the mutineers who originally settled the island. Christian's wife, an aged lady, is a member of this family; her age is not known, but must be great. She states that she distinctly recollects seeing Captain Cook at the three different voyages on which he visited Tahiti. She yet takes a very active part in domestic affairs. The next morning I was awakened at an early hour by the voice of singing, and found the family engaged in their morning devotions. I felt happy that my lot was again cast in a family where the voice of prayer and praise is heard with the departing day, and at morning dawn. The devotions did not seem like a mere form and repetition of words; there was life and pious zeal. As we early left the house, we heard, as we passed along, in every habitation the voice of prayer and praise, which told us that all were engaged with the morning sacrifice. This I may say truly, every house is a nouse of prayer, and their blameless lives evince that every heart is a fit temple of the Holy Spirit."

13*

"There are on the island twelve dwelling-houses, and the church, which is also used for the school-house. The houses are very comfortable, being usually one story high; the roofs covered like the houses in Tahiti, with the ehallah leaves. They are from twenty-five to fifty feet long, at one end they have a small room, which is furnished with a small library, and serves as a retreat during their leisure time, which they spend in reading. They are neat about their dwellings, which are furnished with smooth floors of planed boards. They make cloth from a native tree which forms their principal bedding. They raise yams and potatoes on their plantations in great abundance and of excellent quality. They are cultivating a variety of fruits and vegetables, and in a few years it will be a delightful island, supplied not only with the rich fruit of the tropics, but those of higher latitudes. They take much pride in the cultivation of their lands, which, being very rich, yield plentifully and are of easy cultivation.

"The island is well stocked with fowls and goats, and besides those which are domesticated there are great numbers running wild on the mountains. There is much timber on the island, of various kinds, and much of which looks very fine, and would do well for cabinet work. They have plenty of cocoa-nuts, small, but very sweet. Probably this island affords a greater variety of vegetables and fruits than any other island in these seas. The Banian tree is found here, in several places. One which I saw probably covers several acres. [The reader will notice that one appears in the view of Adams's residence, in the engraving on page 121.] They raise and manufacture sugar and molasses, and seem to be supplied by a bountiful Providence with all the luxuries of life.

"Mr. Nobbs officiated [on the Sabbath which the writer spent there] and they went through with the forms of the Church of England, and a short sermon by Mr. Nobbs, from the words of our Saviour, "Come unto me all ye that labor and are heavy laden, and I will give you rest;' words to all the lovers of Christ unspeakably dear. The people were nearly all present, old and young, all dressed plain and neat."

The young man, from whose manuscript journal the above account is drawn, is the one who brought from the island the Bible that was mentioned in the eleventh chapter, and gave it to Mr. Lord. It was found in the possession of the aged widow of Fletcher Christian; a small duodecimo in fine print, published at Edinburgh more than a century ago; having Tate and Brady's version of the Psalms bound in it. As she could not read it without great difficulty, on account of the smallness of the letters, she proposed to the young man to exchange it for one more convenient to her; an exchange which he gladly made. This is the Bible which the Rev. Mr. Rogers, in his interesting speech before the Seamen's Friends' Society, at New York, in May, 1844, exhibited as "the identical Bible which Adams and his companions retained in their ocean home."

A youth, who had been apprenticed to an apothecary at Lowell, Massachusetts, and had become dissatisfied and restless, ran away and went on board a whaling vessel; in the year 1842 he was at Pitcairn's Island. He attended several of the religious meetings, and being exceedingly vile, he attempted to lead astray one of the young women. She not only resisted his wiles, but conversed with him so faithfully, solemnly, and happily, on the subject of personal religion, that when he got out to sea, he could not throw off the impression made on his mind. He became deeply anxious for the salvation of his soul, and finally found peace in believing on Jesus Christ, and united with the Mariner's Church in Boston.

More than sixty years have now passed away since the landing of the mutineers upon Pitcairn's Island. For nearly ten years they were a prey to their own vices. Oppression and violences, drunkenness and murder, prevailed, until all but Young and Adams had fallen. Young survived but a year after he and Adams, in self-defence, had killed Quintal. During this time they read the church service on the Sabbath, and began to instruct the children. After the death of Young, the responsibility of training that youthful community fell upon Adams. How he met this responsibility we have seen in the preceding volume. By inculcating the truths of the Bible upon the minds of these children, he laid the foundations of a most interesting Christian community, and there, upon that isolated rock, in the midst of the ocean, are the results of his labors. His commission to give religious instruction he received from God, and by the fruits of the tree which was planted by his hand we must judge of its quality. The community has increased to one hundred and seventy persons, who are divided into twenty-one families. They are strictly honest in their dealings with each other, and with those who visit them. They have no locks upon their houses, and those who trade with them do not deem it necessary to witness the measurement of articles purchased from them. Their occupation consists principally in cultivating their land. They rise early, and go about their work diligently. Before commencing the day's work, each family has religious worship, consisting of the reading of two chapters in the Bible, and prayer. Their deportment is always civil. "It is impossible," says a late visitor to the island, "to describe the charm that the society of these islanders throws around them. Greatly to their credit, the men behave in the most exemplary manner." One rough *seaman*, whom I spoke to in praise of such conduct, said, "*Sir, I expect that if one of our fellows was to misbehave himself here, we should not leave him alive.*" The same visitor says, "They are guileless and unsophisticated beyond description." It is a principle with them never to let the sun go down upon their wrath.

They have a regular government, and a most excellent system of laws. At the commencement of each year they elect (by general vote of males and females, over eighteen years of age) a chief magistrate. Two *councillors* are chosen at the same time, one by the magistrate, the other by the people. When any question in dispute cannot be settled by the magistrate, or by the magistrate and councillors, it is referred to a jury of seven. The office of magistrate is not coveted, and it sometimes happens that the individual chosen to this honorable place will kill a hog for the public good rather than accept the office.

The magistrate is to convene the public upon occasions of complaint being made to him; and, on hearing both sides of the question, to commit it to a jury. He is to see all fines levied, and all public works executed; and every one is to treat him with respect. He is not to assume any power or authority on his own responsibility, or without the consent of the majority of the people. In relation to traffic in intoxicating drinks, the principle of the "Maine law" seems to have been substantially adopted. The following is their law: *No person or persons shall be allowed to get spirits of any sort from any vessel, or sell it to strangers, or any person upon the island. No intoxicating liquor shall be taken on shore, unless for medicinal purposes. Any person found guilty of transgressing this law shall be severely punished.*

The following is their law in relation to schools: *There must be a school kept, to which all parents shall be obliged to send their children, who must previously be able to repeat the alphabet, and be of the age of from six to sixteen. The school hours shall be from 7 o'clock in the morning until noon, on all days except Saturdays and Sundays. One shilling, or an equivalent, shall be paid per month by the parents, whether the child attend or not.*

Their school-house is a substantial building, fifty-six feet long and twenty wide. It is furnished with desks, slates, books and maps. The school duties commence with prayer and praise, and conclude with the same.

The village library is distributed among all the families, so that when visiting each other they can have ready access to a book.

Upon the Sabbath they have two religious services, at which all are present who can be. These services are held in the school-house. Their minister, Rev. George H. Nobbs, is a native of Ireland. In his youth he was a seaman, and was appointed midshipman in the British navy. He afterwards held a commission in the Chilian service, and distinguished himself for his bravery. He was once condemned to be shot, but escaped by setting fire to the hut in which he was confined. He was again taken, and again escaped. After many hardships and dangers, he quitted the Chilian service, and went to England. The commander of the ship in which he sailed gave him such an account of the people of Pitcairn Island, that he determined to go there, and in 1826 he set out. He had been four times around the world, and an experience of hardships and sufferings had led him to desire "a life of peace and usefulness to his fellow-creatures." When he arrived at the island, he was received with kindness, and after the death of John Adams, in 1829, was appointed their spiritual teacher. In this capacity he seems to have labored faithfully and successfully, and to have secured the confidence and affection of the people. In 1852 he went to England, in order to receive ordination. He was ordained after the forms of the church of England, and returned to his field. *Before* his ordination, he had labored acceptably and successfully between eighteen and nineteen years. Like his predecessor in the spiritual office, John Adams, who was never formally ordained, he seems to have been blessed in his work. Says a visitor, who heard him officiate, "Mr. Nobbs officiated impressively and earnestly. The most solemn attention was paid by all. They sang two hymns in most magnificent style; and really I have never heard any church singing in any part of the world that could equal it, except at cathedrals."

CONCLUSION.

It is impossible to read thus far this singular history without its awakening some interesting reflections.

1. The careful reader will have noticed that *intoxicating drink* was a very prominent cause of the dreadful tragedy which this book records. The Bounty was furnished with *grog*, which was daily dealt out to the crew. One officer, the surgeon, "was in a constant state of intoxication," and *died* from the effects of intemperance and indolence. The provocation which led to the mutiny was language such as only a man partially intoxicated would be likely to use. Captain Bligh, having called his men scoundrels and thieves, added, with an oath, "You rascals, I'll make you jump overboard!" and then ordered the clerk to "stop the villains' grog." After the mutineers had forced such of the seamen into the boat as they intended to send adrift, and before the officers were put overboard, *a dram was served*, by order of Fletcher Christian. When they were settled at Pitcairn's Island, two of the mutineers constructed a distillery, by which they procured the means of intoxication; and one of them, in a fit of delirium, threw himself from a high rock, and was killed on the spot. Had there been no grog in that ship, how different would probably have been the results of the voyage!

2. What evils come upon men in consequence of not controlling their temper! This is illustrated in the history of Fletcher Christian.

His parents and family connections, who lived in the northern part of England, are said to have been very respectable. He had enjoyed considerable advantages for improvement in knowledge. His abilities were very good. He easily gained distinction in his business as a seaman, and was in a fair way, apparently, to rise in the English navy, and finally be appointed to some high and honorable command. But he had not learned to command his own temper. The treatment he received from the master of the ship aroused his anger, and he foolishly and wickedly gave way to it. Led on by his passion he committed a crime which involved all the guilt of murder, deliberately throwing to the winds and the waves, nineteen of his fellow beings. After this he dared not return to his friends or country, but forced himself into banishment upon a desert island. Thus by one hasty deed under the impulse of anger, he blasted his character and happiness forever!

But he would not have done this, had he learned while young to govern his temper and his pride. Remember, my son, "*A furious man aboundeth in transgression. A man's pride shall bring him low: but honor shall uphold the humble in spirit. Be not hasty in thy spirit to be angry; for anger resteth in the bosom of fools.*"

3. How little the mutineers gained by their wicked course! and what an impressive lesson of admonition is here furnished for seamen. The men who joined in the mutiny probably expected that they should live to enjoy much happiness. They intended to settle in some part of the world, where the hand of justice could not find them, and there pass their days in ease and pleasure. They forgot that there is a God in the heavens, whose eye is ever upon the wicked, and whose providence will sooner or later bring them to punishment. But they could not escape the vengeance that follows crime. Some of them were seized, tried, and executed by the laws of the nation. Some of them were suddenly buried in the bottomless ocean. Some of them were murdered in mutual quarrels. One of them was driven to madness by intemperance and destroyed himself. The ringleader was never happy after his rash deed, but always (as Aleck stated to Captain Pipon,) sullen and morose, and committed so many acts of cruelty as to incur the hatred of his associates, and was murdered by one of the Tahitian servants within two years after landing on Pitcairn's Island. Only one, who seems to have become a penitent, was spared to find any real enjoyment of life.

"*He that formed the eye, shall he not see?—His eyes are upon the ways of man, and he seeth all his goings. There is no darkness nor shadow of death, where the workers of iniquity may hide themselves.*"

4. Again, how the wickedness of Christian and his associates was overruled by God, so that much good has resulted. A fertile island, capable of supporting many inhabitants, which had for ages been a desert, has received a thriving colony. Here an interesting community is established, in which industry and good order prevail, and the influence of religion is universally felt. It is to be hoped that many generations will enjoy these blessings. It is also a remarkable fact, that several persons, before thoughtless, have been awakened, by what they saw and heard in visiting this island, to ask "what shall we do to be saved," and have become hopefully pious. This good was no part of the object sought by the mutineers. They meant not so. But God, while he filled them with the bitter fruit of their own devices, made *their crime* an occasion to exercise *his benevolence*, and rendered *their folly* subservient to *his wisdom*.

5. This story shows the value of a *good character*, and how God takes care of the *innocent*. Though Peter Heywood remained on board the Bounty at the time of the mutiny, he had no sympathy with the mutineers. When the Pandora arrived at Tahiti he gave himself up for trial; and when he was tried it was testified that "*he had always a very good character, and was deserving every one's esteem.*" When the ship in which he was confined in irons went to pieces upon the reefs of New Holland, he swam to the shore, a distance of three and a half miles, preserving only his Prayer Book, which he held in his teeth. Many friends became interested in his case, and, though he was condemned, he was promptly pardoned, and subsequently became a distinguished officer in the British navy.

Truly, God did wonderfully preserve him, not only from being drowned when the Pandora was wrecked, but also from being hung as a pirate, through the wrong impressions of Commander Bligh and the mistaken testimony of his officers. Young Heywood appears to have been perfectly conscious of his innocence, and confident that the Almighty would cause it

14

to be somehow attested; and *God will always protect those who deserve it*, (as he wrote to his mother,) or will *make all their trials and sufferings promote their own good.*

6. The happy condition of the village of Pitcairn shows to every one, how desirable and useful it is for families and neighborhoods, that the children should study and regard the Bible. To what is all the order, industry, cheerfulness, thrift and happiness of that village owing? Suppose that Aleck, when the widows and their orphan children were left to his care, had allowed them to live just as they might please, without making the Bible their guide and rule; what would have been the consequences? Do you think that they would have become the lovely and harmonious society which has been described?

If the Bible were regarded as much by all families, neighborhoods, villages, and nations, as it has been under Aleck's patriarchal government, it would be followed by the same delightful results. All the people would be good and happy. But this cannot be the case, unless the children read, and love, and obey the Bible. For those who do not regard the Bible when they are quite young, very seldom pay regard to it when they are grown up to manhood, or when they have advanced to old age.

Now, my dear readers, do you not desire that the family and country, in which you live, should be virtuous and peaceful? Do you not wish to do all you can to make those around you happy? Then take the Bible for your daily teacher and friend. Read it carefully. See what it tells you to feel, and feel so. See what it tells you to do, and do so. If you feel and do as the Bible tells you, you will be happy yourselves and make others happy. Thus you will be wise unto salvation, and if you should die while young, you will be prepared to sing your Redeemer's praises along with youth and children from the little colony of Aleck and from all the islands of the ocean.

7. This narrative shows us what good it may do to give a Bible to a thoughtless sailor.

How happy for Aleck that a Bible was preserved from the Bounty! Perhaps his mother or some kind friend gave him one, just before he sailed from England. Probably he rarely looked into it, until he began to feel himself an outcast on the lonely island. Certain it is, that he had not read it to any good purpose before the mutiny; for if he was not one of the foremost in guilt, he took a very active part, being one of those who stood with arms around Lieutenant Bligh, threatening death to him if he should not keep silence. That Bible was, it is very likely, stowed away in his chest as a thing of little value. But how precious did he find the Bible when he began to come to his right mind! And what could he have done without it? Blessed book! this alone guided him to the Saviour, and taught him that the blood of Jesus cleanseth from all sin. A most remarkable conversion, by the instrumentality of the Bible alone, a Bible carried from London half across the globe, and all the while held only as a worthless thing, and then in the midst of the Pacific ocean it was found by the solitary sinner to be the word of God and the power of God unto salvation! In desolation and loneliness, when all his companions had fallen, "thoughts came to him in visions of the night," and he was troubled so that he could neither eat nor sleep. In this state of mind, he thought of the Bible which had been saved from the Bounty. He made search, and at length found it. He had never been to school, and had learned to read but imperfectly from scraps of paper which he had picked up in the streets of London when a boy. He commenced praying three times a day. He persevered in reading the Scriptures until his mind became enlightened, and Christ was revealed to him as a Saviour. He then commenced instructing the children of the mutineers in the Scriptures, with such results as we have seen.

8. This narrative has a lesson of admonition to shipmasters. The occasion of the mutiny on board of the Bounty was the rash and provoking language of Cap-

tain Bligh. This roused the passions of a portion of the crew, and led to the determination to take the ship. Christian called to his help the men who had been flogged, and were ready to avenge themselves on their commander. Had Captain Bligh, instead of abusing his men, by calling them scoundrels and rascals, and threatening to make them jump overboard, used dignified language, and maintained his authority by such a deportment as would have commanded the respect of the crew, the mutiny would probably not have occurred. Neither oaths nor rough words, nor yet the lash, will produce subordination on shipboard. A dignified deportment, and the respect of the crew, will avail most to establish authority.

9. Young men and boys who are contemplating the marine service can learn some useful lessons from this narrative. On board the Bounty there was intemperance and profanity. Under such an influence, a " degeneracy of morals " was the natural result. " Evil communications corrupt good manners, and the companion of fools shall be destroyed." Let young men who are going to sea look well to the moral influences which are to surround them. On board many ships provisions are made for the intellectual and moral wants of the crew. Boys are furnished with rooms separate from the common apartment, and such commanders are employed as will exert a salutary influence upon youth committed to their care.

10. This volume furnishes a strong argument in favor of efforts for the moral improvement of seamen. In his last days, John Adams expressed his fears that the morals of the Pitcairn Islanders would be corrupted by the influence of wicked sailors. Some years since, a shipmaster repaid the confidence and hospitality of the people, by decoying an unsuspecting female on board his ship, with the promise of carrying her to England, but shamefully left her at one of the Sandwich Islands, friendless and penniless. Seamen of depraved character are hindering, to the extent of their power, the efforts of Christian missionaries in all parts of the world. How important that their character be elevated! Seamen's

Friend Societies are laboring for this result. By sustaining chaplains, furnishing religious reading and Sailor's Homes, and in various other ways, these societies are laboring for the spiritual good of the men who go down to the sea in ships. By these influences, a great change for the better has been wrought. The same truth which wrought such "a marvellous change" in the character of John Adams has been working out its blessed results in the hearts of many seamen; and who will not help forward the good work, until the abundance of the sea shall be converted?

14* L

APPENDIX.

CONTAINING EXTRACTS FROM THE LAWS AND THE REGISTER OF PITCAIRN'S ISLAND.

LAW RESPECTING THE MAGISTRATE.

"The magistrate is to convene the public on occasions of complaints being made to him; and on hearing both sides of the question, commit it to a jury. He is to see all fines levied, and all public works executed; and every one must treat him with respect. He is not to assume any power or authority on his own responsibility, or without the consent of the majority of the people. A public journal shall be kept by the magistrate, and shall from time to time be read; so that no one shall plead ignorance of the law for any crime he may commit. This journal shall be submitted to the inspection of those captains of British men-of-war, which occasionally touch at the island.

"N. B. Every person, from the age of fifteen and upward, shall pay a fine similar to masters of families."

LAWS REGARDING THE SCHOOL.

"There must be a school kept, to which all parents shall be obliged to send their children, who must previously be able to repeat the alphabet, and be of the age of from six to sixteen. Mr. Nobbs shall be placed at the head of the school, assisted by such persons as shall be named by the chief-magistrate. The school-hours shall be from seven o'clock in the morning until noon, on all days, excepting Saturdays and Sundays; casualties and sickness excepted. One shilling, or an equivalent, as marked below, shall be paid for each child per month, by the parents, whether the child attend school or not. In case Mr. Nobbs does not attend, the assistant appointed by the chief-magistrate shall receive the salary in proportion to the time Mr. Nobbs is absent.

"Equivalent for money:

	s.	d.*
One barrel of yams, valued at	8	0
One barrel of sweet potatoes	8	0
One barrel of Irish potatoes	12	0
Three good bunches of plantains	4	0
One day's labor	2	0

"The chief-magistrate is to see the labor well performed; and goods which may be given for money shall be delivered, either at the market-place, or at the house of Mr. Nobbs, as he may direct."

LAWS RESPECTING LANDMARKS.

"On the 1st of January, after the magistrate is elected, he shall assemble all those who should be deemed necessary; and with them he is to visit all landmarks that are upon the island, and replace those that are lost. Should anything occur to prevent its accomplishment in the time specified (the 1st of January), the magistrate is bound to see it done the first opportunity."

LAWS FOR TRADING WITH SHIPS.

"*No person or persons shall be allowed to get spirits of any sort, from any vessel, or sell it to strangers, or any person upon the island.* Any one found guilty of so doing shall be punished by fine, or such other punishment as a jury shall determine on. *No intoxicating*

* Four shillings of English money are about equal to one dollar.

liquor whatever shall be allowed to be taken on shore, unless it be for medicinal purposes. Any person found guilty of transgressing this law shall be severely punished by a jury. No females are allowed to go on board a foreign vessel of any size or description, without the permission of the magistrate; and in case the magistrate does not go on board himself, he is to appoint four men to look after the females."

LAWS FOR THE PUBLIC ANVIL, ETC.

"Any person taking the public anvil and public sledge-hammer from the blacksmith's shop, is to take it back after he has done with it; and in case the anvil and sledge-hammer should get lost by his neglecting to take it back, he is to get another anvil and sledge-hammer, and pay a fine of four shillings."

LAWS REGARDING CATS, FOWLS, ETC.

"If a CAT is killed without being positively detected in killing fowls, however strong the suspicion may be, the person killing such cat is obliged, as a penalty, to destroy three hundred rats, whose tails must be submitted for the inspection of the magistrate, by way of proof that the penalty has been paid.

"If a fowl is found destroying the yams or potatoes, the owner of the plantation, after giving due warning, may shoot the fowl, and retain it for his use, and may demand of the owner of such fowl the amount of powder and shot so expended, as well as the fowl. The fowls are all toe-marked.

"Goats, and other quadrupeds, are ear-marked.

"If a pig gets loose from its sty and commits any depredation, the owner is obliged to make good the damage, according to the decision of the magistrate, whose duty it is to survey the injury alleged to be done, and from whose decision a reference, if necessary, may be made to a jury; but the final appeal is to the captain of the next man-of-war touching at the island."

A bank was set on foot a few years since at Pitcairn.

The dollars, which were not very numerous, were allowed to accumulate for a time, partly with the object of purchasing a vessel. But the plan did not answer; and the several deposits were returned.

THE REGISTER OF PITCAIRN'S ISLAND, from 1790 to 1850, is a very interesting document, and will probably be of great value hereafter, as a record of names and events connected with that little world. A few extracts will be given.

The first entry occurs January 23, 1790: "H. M. S. Bounty burned. Fasto, wife of John Williams, died. October Thursday Christian born."

The annals of 1793 are of a most melancholy kind, recounting the massacre of Fletcher Christian, John Mills, William Brown, John Williams, Isaac Martin; and the death of the Tahitian men, "part by jealousy among themselves, and others by the remaining Englishmen."

In 1794 we read of "a great desire in many of the women to leave the island: and of a boat built on purpose to remove them, launched and upset." In August, the same year, "a grave was dug, and the bones of all the white men that had been murdered were buried." In November, "a conspiracy of the women to kill all the white men, when asleep in their beds, was discovered. They were all seized, a disclosure ensued, and all were pardoned." November 30, "the women attacked the white men, but no one was hurt. They were once more pardoned, and threatened the next time with death."

"1795, *May* 6. — The first two canoes, for the purpose of catching fish, were made. Saw a vessel close in with the island. Mutineers much alarmed. Vessel stood out to sea December 27.

"1797. — Endeavored to procure a quantity of meat for salting, and to make syrup from the ti-plant and sugar-cane.

"1799. — Matthew Quintal having threatened to take the lives of Young and Adams, these two considered their lives in danger, and thought they were justified in taking away the life of Quintal, which they did with an axe.

"1800.—Edward Young, a mutineer, died of asthma.

"1817.—Arrived, ship Sultan, of Boston, Captain Reynolds; Jenny, a Tahitian woman, left here in the Sultan.

"1823.—Arrived, ship Cyrus, of London, Captain Hall; John Buffett came on shore, as school-master, and John Evans also came on shore.

"1825, *December* 5.—Arrived, H. M. S. Blossom, Captain F. W. Beechey.

"1826, *December* 19.—Jane Quintal left the island in the Lovely, of London, Captain Blythe.

"1828, *November* 15.—George Nobbs came on shore to reside.

"1829, *March* 5.—

JOHN ADAMS died, aged 65.

"1830, *March* 15.—Arrived, H. M. S. Seringapatam, Captain Hon. W. Waldegrave, with a present of clothes, and agricultural implements and tools, from the British government.

"1831, *February* 28.—Arrived, H. M. Sloop Comet, Alexander A. Sandilands, and bark Lucy Anne, of Sydney, government vessel, J. Currey master, for the purpose of removing the inhabitants of Pitcairn's Island to Tahiti.

"*March* 6.—All the inhabitants embarked and sailed for Tahiti.

"*March* 21.—Soon after our arrival at Tahiti, the Pitcairn people were taken sick.

"1831.—John Buffett and family, Robert Young, Joseph Christian, etc., sailed from Tahiti, in a small schooner; but, owing to contrary winds, they landed at Lord Hood's Island.

"*June* 21.—John Buffett, and the others on Lord Hood's Island, embarked in the French frigate Bordeaux Packet, and on the 27th landed at Pitcairn's Island. During our absence our hogs have gone wild, and destroyed our crops. After we returned, we employed ourselves in destroying the hogs.

"1838, *November* 29.—Arrived, H. M. S. Fly, Captain Russell Elliott, with a present from Rev. Mr. Rowlandson and congregation at Valparaiso. Captain Elliott proposed electing a chief-magistrate, which was adopted; and Edward Quintal was chosen.

"This island was taken possession of by Captain Elliott, on behalf of the Crown of Great Britain, on the 29th of November, 1838.

"1839, *November* 9.—Arrived, H. M. S. Sparrowhawk, Captain J. Shepherd. The captain, several officers, and Gen. Friere, ex-president of Chili, landed. In the afternoon the school-children were examined, and received the approbation of our respected visitors. Captain Shepherd afterward divided some valuable presents among them.

"10.—Captain Shepherd and his officers attended divine service twice. At five P. M. they went on board. They sailed on the 12th.

"1840, *February* 8.—Mrs. Nobbs received a severe contusion on the shoulder, by the falling of a cocoa-nut from the tree.

"*February* 13.—Moses Young fell from a cocoa-nut tree, at least forty feet high, and was but slightly injured.

"1841, *August* 18.—Arrived, H. M. S. Curaçoa, Captain Jenkin Jones; and a most opportune arrival it was, for there were at least twenty cases of influenza among us." The register goes on to describe the valuable services rendered by Captain Jones and the surgeon of the ship, Dr. Gunn. The Curaçoa sailed on the 20th.

"*September* 19.—Died, Isabella, a native of Tahiti, relict of Fletcher Christian, of the Bounty. Her age was not known; but she frequently said she remembered Captain Cook arriving at Tahiti.

"1843, *March* 4.—Eleven of the inhabitants sailed in the bark America, for the purpose of exploring Elizabeth Island.

"5.—Arrived, H. M. S. Talbot, Captain Sir T.

Thompson, Bart. After remaining on shore, and adjusting some of the most pressing judicial cases presented to him, he went on board, and sailed for Valparaiso.

"11.—Bark America returned from Elizabeth Island, our people bringing a very unfavorable report of it.

"1844, *July* 28.—Arrived, H. M. S. Basilisk, Captain Henry Hunt, bringing presents from the British government.

"1845, *January* 19.—During the last week, we have been employed in fishing up two of the Bounty's large guns. For fifty-five years they have been deposited at the bottom of the sea, on a bed of coral, guiltless of blood, during the time so many thousands of mankind became, in Europe, food for cannon. But on Saturday last one of the guns resumed its natural vocation—at least, the innoxious portion of it—to wit, pouring forth fire and smoke, and causing the island to reverberate with its bellowing; the other gun is condemned to silence, having been spiked by some one in the Bounty.

"1845, *April* 16."—The diary of this date contains a striking description of a storm, which, bursting over the island, greatly alarmed the inhabitants. A considerable portion of the earth was detached from the side of the hill situate at the head of a ravine, and carried into the sea; about three hundred cocoa-nut trees were torn up by the roots, and borne along with it; a yam-ground, containing one thousand yams, totally disappeared; several fishing-boats were destroyed, and large pieces of rock were found blocking up the harbor in several parts. In the interior, all the plantain patches were levelled, and about four thousand plantain-trees destroyed, one half in full bearing, the other designed for the year 1846. "So that," says the annalist, "this very valuable article of food we shall be without for a long time. The fact is, that from this date until August we shall be pinched for food. But God tempers the wind to the shorn lamb; and we humbly trust that the late monitions of Providence, namely, drought, sickness, and storm, which severally have afflicted us this year, may be sanctified to us, and be the means of bringing us, one and all, into a closer communion with our God. May we remember the rod, and who hath appointed it! May we flee to the cross of Christ for safety and succor in every time of need, always bearing in mind that our heavenly Father doth not willingly afflict the children of men!"

The details which follow, respecting a serious accident to the pastor's eldest son, Reuben E. Nobbs, which resulted in what appears to be confirmed lameness, are so characteristic of the kind and brotherly feeling subsisting in the island, that they must be quoted in full.

"1847, *February* 20.—This afternoon, as Reuben Nobbs was out in the mountain, shooting goats, his foot slipped, and he let fall his musket, which exploded and wounded him severely. The ball entered a little below the hip-joint, and passing downward, came through on the inside of the thigh, about half-way between the groin and the knee. Providentially, some persons were within call, who immediately ran to his assistance, and tore up their shirts to stanch the blood, which was pouring forth profusely. A lad was despatched to the village with the melancholy news; and in a few minutes the whole of the inhabitants capable of going were on their way to afford relief, headed by his affectionate mother, who was almost frantic with grief. In about an hour they returned, bearing him in a canoe, which they had taken up for that purpose. After some difficulty the blood was stanched, and the lad suffered but little pain. Every person was anxious to render assistance; the greater part of the male inhabitants remained at night, to be ready at a moment's warning to do anything that might be required. Toward midnight he fell asleep; and so ends this melancholy day.

"21.—About daylight the wounded lad awoke, very much refreshed; he does not complain much, and has but little fever. The men and grown lads have formed themselves into three watches, to attend his wants, both day and night. It is most gratifying to his parents to see the esteem in which their son is held.

"22.—Reuben Nobbs is free from pain, but there is a considerable accession of fever; it does not appear that either the thigh or hip bone is injured, as he can

15

move his leg without much difficulty or pain. From the great length of the internal wound, it is difficult to ascertain whether any of the wadding remains where the ball must have passed through.

"26. — This morning a ship was reported; everybody appeared rejoiced, hoping to get some necessaries for their wounded friend. On nearing the island, she proved to be H. M. S. Spy, Captain Wooldridge. 'Thank God!' was the grateful exclamation of many, on hearing it was a ship of war, on account of her having a surgeon on board. At one P. M. Captain Wooldridge and the surgeen (Dr. Bowden) landed, who immediately visited young Nobbs; and after probing the wound, and ascertaining the extent of the injury, gave his opinion that there was not much danger, and that with proper attention he would, in all probability, recover, although a narrower escape from death never came beneath his notice. Captain Wooldridge, being much pressed for time, informed the inhabitants he must sail that evening. After kindly interesting himself in the welfare of the island, and noting down such things as the community were most in want of, at sunset the Spy sailed for Valparaiso.

"*June* 4. — Experienced a heavy gale from the westward, which, if it had been of long duration, would have done incalculable damage. A large piece of the banyan-tree was blown down, and the flag-staff broken in two pieces.

"1848, *March* 9. — Arrived, H. M. S. Calypso, Captain H. Worth.

"10. — At nine A. M. Captain Worth, and a party of officers, landed; and the greeting on both sides was most cordial. Our people, men, women and children, are almost beside themselves."

Many valuable and useful presents were brought to the island. The next day the ship was discovered four miles from the land. Captain Worth, Dr. Domet, and others, again landed. The doctor wishing to inspect the hieroglyphics, carved by the aborigines, went down the face of the cliff without the assistance of a rope — a most hazardous feat. It is stated that he was the first European who had performed it.

" At sunset the Calypso sailed, carrying with her our grateful aspirations," &c.

"1849, *July* 10."—A very animated description is given, under this date, of the arrival of "the Pandora, Captain Wood, from Oahu and Tahiti, bringing us Mr. Buffett back, who left us for the Sandwich Islands last summer.

"*July* 11.—This evening, Captain Wood left us, to our great regret; for though our acquaintance was but of two days' duration, the urbanity of Captain Wood, and his solicitude for our welfare, have made a deep and, we hope, a lasting impression on our hearts. That the good ship Pandora, and all her gallant crew, may escape the perils of the deep, and, before many months have elapsed, show her number some early day at Spithead, is the wish of their friends residing on the rock of the West.

"*August* 9.—The inhabitants are slowly recovering from the epidemic which has pervaded the island during the last month. So general was the attack, that the public school has been discontinued, and public service but once performed on each Sabbath, in consequence; the teacher being fully employed attending the sick.

"11.—Arrived, H. M. S. Daphne, Captain Fanshawe, from Valparaiso, bringing the *desiderata* of the community, viz., a bull, cow, and some rabbits. They were landed without any difficulty by our own boats. We also received from the Rev. Mr. Armstrong several boxes of acceptable articles, and a large case of books from the Society for Promoting Christian Knowledge. At three P. M. Captain Fanshawe and a party of the officers landed. At sunset they returned on board again, except the surgeon, who remained on shore, at the particular request of Mr. Nobbs, who required some advice about the sick.

"12.—At one P. M. Captain Fanshawe returned on shore, with a fresh party of officers, and attended divine service. Much persuasion was used by our young people to induce Captain F. to remain another day, but he told them he could not do so with propriety. At sunset they all returned on board, and H. M. S. Daphne sailed for Tahiti. Captain F. (as well as his officers) treated those of our people who went on board most kindly, and made most minute inquiries into our wants and actual condition. They were pleased to express their satisfaction at what they saw and heard, and left us deeply impressed with their courtesy and urbanity. May Almighty God have them in his holy keeping!

"*September* 6 — A large hair-seal captured on the west side of the island. Fletcher Christian first discovered it among the rocks, and was much alarmed at the sight of it. He feared to go near it, lest it should be a ghost (of which he has a great horror), or some beast of prey; but quickly ascended the hill which overlooks the town, and gave the alarm. Some persons went over to his assistance, and shot the animal just as it was making its retreat into the sea.

"20. — *This day was set apart as a day of fasting and prayer.* Public service commenced at eleven A. M., and ended at one P. M. All who could get to church attended. Text, Romans ii. 4, 5. One of the females fainted during service."

"SUMMARY.

"This year is unprecedented in the annals of Pitcairn's Island. We have been visited by two British men-of-war, the Pandora, Captain Wood, and the Daphne, Captain Fanshawe. The commanders of these ships, and their officers, treated the inhabitants with the greatest kindness, and were pleased to express their entire approval of all they saw and heard. Another (to us) wonderful occurrence is the arrival of so many other ships under English colors, viz., eight from the Australian colonies, bound for California, and one whaling vessel from London; in all, nine merchantmen and two ships of war. American ships have dwindled down to six whalers and one from California; in her, Reuben E. Nobbs embarked for Valparaiso.

"George Adams saved the life of a child alongside of a ship in the offing.

"The inhabitants, with scarcely one exception, have suffered from sickness very severely during the months of August, September, and October. The school was discontinued, the children being too sick to attend, and the teacher was fully (and, thank God! efficiently) employed in ministering from house to house. Some of the cases were quite alarming, and the disease (the influenza) in general was more severe, but considerably modified from that of former years; violent spasms in the stomach and epigastric region were frequent in all stages of the complaint. At the close of the year, the inhabitants are enjoying much better health. May the recent affliction teach us so to number our days that we may apply our hearts unto wisdom!"

"1850, *January* 23. — This day was observed as the anniversary of the settlement of this colony, sixty years since. One survivor of that strange event, and sanguinary result, witnessed its celebration. At daylight one of the Bounty's guns was discharged, and awakened the sleeping echoes and the more drowsy of its inhabitants. At ten A. M. divine service was performed. After the service, various letters received from the British government and principal friends were read, and commented upon. At twelve o'clock (noon), a number of musketeers assembled under the flag-staff, and fired a volley in honor of the day. After dinner, males and females assembled in front of the church (where the British flag was flying), and gave three cheers for Queen Victoria, three for the government at home, three for the magistrate here, three for absent friends, three for the ladies, and three for the community in general, amid the firing of muskets and ringing of the bell. At sunset, the gun of the Bounty was again fired, and the day closed in harmony and peace, both toward God and man. It is voted that an annual celebration be observed.

"1850, *March* 24. — Daniel McCoy and Lydia Young married.

"*June* 3. — John Pitcairns Elford (native of Adelaide, New South Wales) baptized.

"*July* 15. — Susannah (a native of Tahiti, and last

15*

survivor of the Bounty) died from the prevailing epidemic and the exhaustion of old age combined.

"*September* 27. — Mrs. Eliza C. Palmer, wife of George Palmer, of Nantucket, died of consumption.

"28. — Edward Quintal (second) fell from the precipice upon the rocks below, and badly fractured his leg.

"*December* 14. — Charles William Grant born, son of the master of a whaler, whose wife had been left on the island.

"1851, *January* 1. — Thursday O. Christian elected chief-magistrate. John Buffett, Jr., and Thomas Buffett, counsellors.

"23. — Observed the anniversary of the settlement of the colony. David Buffett and Martha Young married.

"*March* 15. — By the accidental discharge of a fowling-piece in a whale-boat that was out fishing, three persons, viz., Abraham Quintal, John Buffett, and Fletcher Nobbs, were seriously injured.

"*August* 16. — Twelve of the inhabitants sailed in the Joseph Meigs for the purpose of visiting Elizabeth Island. On their arrival at the island they discovered a human skeleton; and as nothing could be found that may lead to discover who this unfortunate individual was, it must remain a mystery.

"*November* 11. — Thirty-eight of the inhabitants sailed in the ship Sharon, of Fairhaven, for the purpose of visiting Elizabeth Island. On Friday, 14th, after a boisterous passage of three days, they landed upon Elizabeth Island, when they immediately set about wooding the ship, and exploring the country, which is evidently of coral formation. The soil is very scanty, and totally unfit for cultivation. Various specimens of marine shells are dispersed all over the surface of the island, which, in combination with the thickly scattered pieces of coral, renders travelling both difficult and dangerous. Water is found on the north-west part of the island slowly dripping from the roof of a cave, which cannot be reached without the aid of ropes. The island rises about sixty feet above the level of the sea. Eight human skeletons were also found upon the island, lying in caves. They were doubtless the remains of some unfortunate shipwrecked seamen, as several pieces of a wreck were found upon the shore.

"1852, *January* 2. — Abraham B. Quintal elected chief-magistrate; Frederick Young and David Buffett, counsellors.

"*April* 5. — Fletcher Christian died, after a lingering illness of many months' duration, aged forty years. As a member of the community, the conduct of Fletcher Christian was ever worthy of imitation; suffice it to say, that his many amiable and agreeable qualities will cause his memory long to be cherished by those he has left behind."

The following returns of births, deaths, and marriages, and some other particulars, have been drawn chiefly from the authentic statements in the Register of the Island:

"1845. — Births, 7; deaths, 0; marriages, 2: males, 65; females, 62; total, 127: 51 children attend the school.

"1846. — Births, 7; death, 1; marriages, 0: males, 69; females, 65: total, 134: 47 children attend public school.

"1847. — Births, 6; deaths, 0; marriages, 0: males, 72; females, 68; total, 140: 48 children attend the school.

"1848. — Births, 7; death, 1; marriages, 3: males, 74; females, 72; total, 146: 44 children attend the school; 30 scholars, of 14 years old and upward, attend the Sunday-school. The attendance at the Wednesday Bible-class for adults quite satisfactory.

"1849. — Births, 10; death, 1; marriage, 1: males, 76; females, 79; total, 155: 47 children attend the school, 30 the Sunday-school.

"1850. — Births, 4; deaths, 3; marriage, 1: inhabitants, 156: males, 79; females, 76. Number of ships touching here, 47: American, 29; English, 17; Hanoverian, 1.

"1851. — Births, 12; deaths, 2; marriages, 3: inhabitants, 166: 81 females, and 85 males. Number of ships touching here, 24: American, 18; English, 6.

"1852. — the number of inhabitants is now 170: 88 males; 82 females."

About 330 vessels have touched at Pitcairn since 1808.

Zeitfracht Medien GmbH
Ferdinand-Jühlke-Straße 7
99095 Erfurt, Deutschland
produktsicherheit@kolibri360.de